THE AUTHOR ·

Don W. Basham was born and reared in Wichita Falls, Texas. In 1951 he left a promising career in commercial art in that city to enter the Christian ministry. He holds the B.A. and B.D. degrees from Phillips University and its Graduate Seminary in Enid, Oklahoma, and is an ordained minister in the Christian Church (Disciples of Christ).

Following a five-year pastorate in suburban Washington, D.C., he became pastor of the Hillcrest Christian Church in Toronto, Canada. With his wife, Alice, and their five children, Mr. Basham currently makes his home in Pampano Beach, Florida. In addition to this book, his writings include articles published in Christian Life magazine and various other religious periodicals.

Face up with a miracle

Don Basham

WHITAKER BOOKS
607 LAUREL DRIVE
MONROEVILLE, Pa. 15146
Phone 412-372-6420

HARDBOUND
First printing August, 1967
Second printing October, 1967
Third printing January, 1968
Fourth printing August, 1968
Fifth printing February, 1969

PAPERBACK
First printing March, 1969—30,000 copies
Second printing September, 1969—20,000 copies
Third printing February, 1970—20,000 copies
Fourth printing July, 1970—25,000 copies
Fifth printing October, 1970—25,000 copies

WHITAKER BOOKS
First printing May, 1971—25,000 copies
Second printing December, 1971—25,000 copies

Contents

Introduction

Is GOD TRULY ALIVE and, if so, is He interested in injecting Himself into the lives of those who believe in Him?

This is the basic question facing man in the last half of the twentieth century.

The National Council of Churches surveyed delegates to a recent Biennial Assembly with surprising results. On the Biblical account of the virgin birth of Jesus, only 28 percent of the delegates replied that they believed that it was "completely true." Likewise, only 19 percent said they believed the Biblical account of Jesus walking on water was "completely true." On present day miracles, 25 percent believed they could happen just as the Bible said. A larger group—35 percent—held that miracles could happen but could be explained by natural causes.

The staggering fact is that two-thirds of the delegates responding to these questions were ordained clergymen and 45 percent were staff members for denominations or councils of churches.

Regrettably, this unwillingness to accept God as being alive in our day is not limited to the black-robed theologians of the more liberal churches. They appear to have their counterparts in many areas of evangelical Christianity, where doctrinal deviations and Scriptural delineations are propounded to claim that miracles are not for our day.

Yet in every age God has raised up men and women who were able to simply believe Him and allow Him to demonstrate His mighty power. Don Basham is one of these men in our day. The record which he has given us here of his journey of faith is both simple and profound. Its simplicity stems from the fact that though a minister of the Christian Church, Basham is willing to honestly portray the doubts and fears which beset him in his early days of struggle for a meaningful faith. The account is profound because, having read it, the reader is faced squarely with the question, "If this could happen to one man or one church, what would happen if ministers and churches everywhere would similarly take God at His word?"

Granted, this is a record of a single minister. But as remarkable as it is, Basham's account does not stand alone. Not a single historical denomination today is without similar men. These are men who honestly faced the fact that if God isn't alive and able to perform miracles in our day, their church was helpless and their profession hopeless. Then they discovered that to those who come to Him in simple believing humility, God can and does reveal Himself in mighty astonishing power.

Clearly, there is hope for our day. But this hope is not in the organization, man power or finances of the church. It is in the person of Jesus Christ, the Son of the Living God, who when He left the scene of this earth said, *"He that believeth on me, the works that I do shall he do also; and greater works than these shall he do; because I go unto my Father"* (John 14:12).

Robert Walker
Editor of *Christian Life* magazine

Preface

The ultimate thing which anyone can say about the Living God is, "I have encountered Him; He has reached me. He stood at my door and knocked, and when I opened the door, He came in and communed with me." The person who provides such a witness could be wrong, he could be lying—but his is the ultimate evidence.[1]

ONCE, AFTER I SPOKE on the power of prayer, a woman came to me and said, "I believe you, for you are the first minister I ever heard who said, 'I know this is true because it has happened to me.' "

Experience is always more vital than theory, and nowhere is this more true than in the religious realm. There is no adequate substitute for personal testimony. It is this fact which leads me to share the story of my own spiritual quest. It is not that my story is so very unique, but I trust that my witness, when added to the weight of others, may encourage many who have not yet begun exploring the life of faith—and those who have begun but have yet to share their findings.

Such testimony is not overly common among ministers. Ministers lean more to writing books of sermons or scholarly works defending their theology or curriculum materials for their denominations. The observant layman has often noted how the minister tends to defend the faith like a lawyer defending a client, without getting personally involved.

But in this day of rising skepticism there is a crying

1. Elton Trueblood, in *The Company of the Committed*, page 59; Harper and Row, N.Y., N.Y., used by permission.

need for the testimony of those who are personally involved in their proclamation of the faith. I agree with Dr. Frank Laubach who wrote:

> In defense of opening my soul and laying it bare to the public gaze in this fashion, I may say that it seems to me that we really seldom do anybody much good excepting as we share the deepest experiences of our souls in this way. It is not the fashion to tell your inmost thoughts, but there are many wrong fashions, and concealment of the best in us is wrong. I disapprove of the usual practice of talking "small talk" whenever we meet, and holding a veil over our souls. If we are so impoverished that we have nothing to reveal but small talk, then we need to struggle for more richness of soul. As for me, I am convinced that this spiritual pilgrimage which I am making is infinitely worthwhile, the most important thing I know of to talk about. And talk I shall while there is anybody to listen. And I hunger—O how I hunger!—for others to tell me their soul adventures.[2]

As far back as I can remember I have belonged to the "I Hope There's Something More" category of persons. That is, I *wanted* to believe. As a child the stories I heard or read about God doing wonderful things for people stirred me. Like the time the lady who lived down the street had a husband who was very ill. The doctors said he would die, but one night while she was praying in her back yard, Jesus appeared in the moonlight and said her husband would live. *And he did.*

Nor was I more than about seven years old the time some of my friends came home from Sunday school arguing whether Peter really walked on the water when Jesus told him he could. I don't recall who won the argument, but the Bible story stuck in my mind. A few days later, after a hard summer shower, I stood barefoot in the middle of a dirt street, with the cool mud oozing between my toes, staring at a large puddle of water which stretched across a low place in the street. I felt an almost irresistible

2. Frank C. Laubach, in *Letters by a Modern Mystic*, page 11, used by permission.

yearning to try walking on top of that puddle instead of wading through it.

In a way that childhood experience proved prophetic. Eventually I was to learn how our Christian faith can furnish the power which enables us to walk on top of life instead of just wading through it; and when, like Peter, we began to sink and cry out for help, how God is there to deliver us by His miraculous power.

So if you're sure you can't believe in miracles, you may want to stop right here; for this book is about miracles and the God who performs them.

Don W. Basham

PREFACE TO PAPERBACK EDITION

EIGHTEEN MONTHS HAVE PASSED since *Face Up with a Miracle* first appeared in the bookstores. The public's response has been warm and enthusiastic. By the end of the first year the book was headed for its fourth printing in hardcover, and by the time this new paperback edition makes its debut, the fifth hardcover edition will also be in circulation.

The publication of the book has resulted in some profound changes in my life and ministry. As distribution of the book increased I began to receive many invitations to minister in various cities across the country. Whenever possible I accepted those invitations, but soon a real conflict of ministries became evident. I could not continue to accept out-of-town invitations to speak without neglecting my responsibilities to the congregation which had called me as its minister, which paid my salary and which had first claim on my time. I was faced with the necessity of making a crucial decision. Either I would have to refuse the increasing number of invitations and settle down to the routine work of the pastorate, or resign from the pastorate and step out in faith through the many new doors which beckoned so appealingly. But such a drastic change as leaving the pastorate meant facing a whole new set of problems and fears. Could I give up the security of my salary, parsonage, pension and allowances which had provided for the economic needs of my family for nearly fifteen years? Would God make good His word and provide fully for our needs?

I did not doubt His ability to provide so much as I

doubted my ability to trust Him. I suddenly saw that it was one thing to stand in the midst of material security and preach to others about God meeting the needs of those who ask and trust Him, and quite another thing to decide to step out in faith and discover for myself whether His promises could be trusted on a day-to-day basis. I would be less than honest if I said the choice was an easy one. It was not. But we made it anyway.

After long hours of discussion and prayer, my wife and I moved in the only direction we could move and still maintain the integrity of our witness. We agreed that we would step out in faith and trust God. So with fear and trembling, yet in great spiritual excitement, I resigned as minister of the East Side Church in Sharon, Pennsylvania and we moved to our present home in Pompano Beach, Florida. A year has passed since that decision, and it has been the most rewarding year of my life. We have experienced marvelous and repeated assurances of God's love and provision. We have found God does make good His word! There have been many testings, and more than once I have had to wrestle against fear and Satan's accusing voice, but God is faithful—He has met our every need.

Significantly enough, things have not gone quite like I anticipated. Some doors of opportunity which seemed to be opening at the time I resigned never really opened. Other doors God has kept tightly shut. But—oh!—the unthought of, unexpected doors which He has opened, giving me opportunity to minister in places I never dreamed of, both in this country and overseas! Also, in addition to my travels, I have completed the manuscript of a second book, to be published in the fall of 1969, and am well into the writing of a third. The miracles I hear of and see happening mount faster than I can write about them.

As for the ministry of *Face Up with a Miracle*, we continue to be amazed and humbly grateful. Without the anointing of the Holy Spirit, the book is simply a testimony of the Christian experiences of a single family, but the Holy Spirit seems to accompany it in a way which brings great blessing. One of the most amazing reports which has come to us is that of an alcoholic who, facing ruin and a broken family, drank three fifths of whiskey as he sat reading the book and remained sober as a judge. As he finished the book God delivered him from alcohol and now he is becoming a spiritual leader in his community.

As *Face Up with a Miracle* makes its appearance in this inexpensive and easy-to-share edition, we recommit its testimony to the Lord Jesus Christ who made it possible and pray that His Holy Spirit will continue to use it to reach additional multitudes who may be helped and blessed by its message.

Don W. Basham
441 N.E. 2nd Street
Pompano Beach, Fla.
33060

To Alice

CHAPTER ONE

The Day That Changed Our Lives

THE DAY THAT CHANGED OUR LIVES began in an ordinary way. It was just another summer Sunday morning, and Alice and I drove to church to take our usual places in the choir. We had met and married in church—the First Christian Church of Wichita Falls, Texas—and it was like a second home to us. Our friends were church friends and our interests church interests. With no worldly ambitions beyond that of a modest career in commercial art, we began our marriage fully expecting to live and die right there in our home town. But Sunday changed all that.

I'm sure the ground work for what happened had already been laid—partly by our own spiritual restlessness. For in spite of our busy church life, we felt something was missing. Reading the Bible together hadn't helped much either—except to raise some disturbing questions. What does it mean to be "born again"? How much of the New Testament should a modern Christian believe? What did Jesus mean when He said, "Whoever would save his life will lose it, and whoever loses his life for my sake will find it"?

Nothing in our church activities threw light on such questions and our attempts to discuss them with our friends got us exactly nowhere. "Don't be so serious! You're good church members—what more do you want? Leave the questions up to the experts. If you don't, first thing you know you'll turn into a couple of fanatics!"

Since our friends were so content with things as they were, we often wondered if there was something wrong with us. Besides, we weren't even sure ourselves what we were looking for. Maybe it didn't even exist.

The minister's sermon that morning only added to our discontent. He described the New Testament Church and the early Christians. They were people who were on fire for their faith, he said, people who knew the Holy Spirit guided and directed their lives. Then he asked why we shouldn't have that same kind of dynamic fellowship. And for a little while—at least while he was preaching—I desperately wished that we could. I wanted that kind of life and that kind of power! But then the sermon ended.

An invitation hymn was sung but no one responded. Following the benediction people picked up and left, smiling and chatting among themselves as if nothing had happened—just like they did Sunday after Sunday. Church was over for another week.

The organ postlude died away as we left the choir loft and made our way back to the robing room. There was a crowd around the closets and we stood waiting our turn to leave our robes.

"How can people hear a great sermon like that and not realize . . ." I began, only to leave the unfinished sentence hanging alongside our choir robes. Elbowing our way out of the room, down the church corridor and out into the bright Texas sunlight, we had climbed into our car and begun poking our way slowly along the crowded street before Alice replied.

"I know what you didn't finish saying back there," she sighed, and counting on her fingers she ticked off the phrases. "Lovely day, large crowd, inspiring service, tremendous sermon, and then . . . *phfft!* It's all over and we all go home. Nothing's different and no one is changed." She let her hands fall in her lap. I nodded. Surely, we agreed, the Christian faith has something more to offer.

It has, and we were on the verge of finding it out.

After dinner we drove to the hospital to visit a friend who was awaiting surgery. "Room number for Mrs.

Dorothy Hollister, please." We watched the reception-ist's nimble fingers flick through the registration cards. After going through them a second time she glanced up.

"Sorry, we have no Mrs. Hollister. Are you sure you have the right hospital?"

"She was admitted Wednesday and scheduled for surgery tomorrow morning," I explained. "She must be here."

"Let me check the dismissals." The receptionist dis-appeared into a nearby office and returned with a list at-tached to a clip board. "Here she is," she announced. "Your Mrs. Hollister has been dismissed."

"Dismissed? But she was scheduled for surgery to-morrow."

The receptionist shook her head. "I can't help that, sir. The record is right here. Mrs. Hollister was sent home this morning."

We left the hospital and drove in the direction of Dorothy's house. "What do you suppose happened?" Alice asked.

"There's one way to find out," I answered, not know-ing the story we were to hear would change the very di-rection of our lives. Minutes later I rang the doorbell and found Dorothy expecting us.

"Come in and let me tell you what happened." Her face glowed with joy and excitement as she led the way into her living room and motioned us toward the sofa.

"You know how ill I was when I entered the hospital Wednesday," she began. We nodded and listened with fascination as her story unfolded. Suffering from a gall bladder condition, she lay in the hospital bed for two days, shot full of sedatives to help alleviate the excruciat-ing pain. Tests clearly indicated her condition called for surgery, which—as we had heard—was scheduled for Monday. But on Friday a little neighbor lady slipped into her room long enough to make a surprising request. Would Dorothy mind if she got in touch with her minister to bring him and some church friends to pray for her re-covery?

"As much pain as I had," Dorothy continued, "I was ready to try anything. Besides, she is my neighbor and I didn't want to offend her." So later that day the neighbor returned with her minister and friends. Crowding into Dorothy's room, they began to pray for her healing.

"I was startled and almost angry at first," Dorothy admitted. "They were so *noisy!* All praying out loud and at the same time. I was really wishing they would leave, when all at once *Something* came over me . . . a kind of feeling. No, it was more than a feeling. Oh, I simply can't describe it. But suddenly I found myself sitting up in bed, my body tingling all over, and I felt marvelous! The pain was gone. I was well!"

She paused and fumbled for a handkerchief to wipe at the tears which had suddenly appeared in her eyes. "God answered their prayers and healed me," she said in a voice so low we could scarcely hear. I swallowed hard against the lump in my own throat. A glance toward Alice revealed she was close to tears as well. Dorothy concluded her story saying that her doctor, baffled by the sudden change in her condition, had re-examined her thoroughly. Then, after another day of observation and further tests, he had sent her home.

We sat in silence for awhile with Dorothy smiling at us through her tears. Then slowly it began to dawn on me; we had come face up with a miracle! Here was the kind of experience which happens only in books or to strangers in far away places. But not this time. This time it was close to home. We were face-to-face with living proof of God's miracle-working power.

We drove home deeply moved by Dorothy's testimony. Didn't the Bible say somewhere, "Jesus Christ is the same yesterday, today and forever?" [1] Of course it did. What we had suspected was now confirmed. The church had scarcely touched the immense power latent in the Christian faith! That night the Christ whom we had worshipped from a distance became the personal, living Lord of our lives. For the first time, as we prayed, we felt the

1. Hebrews 13:8

magnificent, silent benediction of the Holy Spirit. His loving presence was unmistakable, and from the center of that Presence a silent command seemed to issue. "Seek ye first the kingdom of God . . ." [2]

The next morning the whole world was a different place. "Do you suppose this is what Jesus meant by saying we must be 'born again'?" I asked Alice. It proved precisely that for both of us—although not yet fully grasping the "doctrine" of it, we had been "born of the Spirit" [3] through faith in a *living* Christ.

2. Matthew 6:33
3. John 3:5,6

CHAPTER TWO

A Different Kind of Christian

WE HAD NOW COME ACROSS a completely different type of Christian. While noisily enthusiastic about their faith, they demonstrated a power in prayer which was remarkable. "Pentecostals" they called themselves. We found that the people who prayed for Dorothy's healing belonged to a pentecostal church.

Like most folk, we had heard just enough about the pentecostals—or "Holy Rollers" as they were often called—to know that whatever they thought they had, it wasn't Christianity. It couldn't be; it was too undignified! They were just emotional fanatics who enjoyed a shouting good time and called it Christianity. Yet it had been these same "fanatics" who demonstrated the love and concern to come and pray for our friend. Now we began to see these earnest, misunderstood people in a whole new light.

The pentecostal Christians attributed their power in prayer to a peculiar experience called the "baptism in the Holy Spirit" which was, they claimed, a spiritual experience beyond conversion or rebirth, and one which equipped them for powerful Christian service. "When you receive this baptism," they told us, "the unmistakable sign is that you speak in 'unknown tongues'—languages you never learned."

It all sounded very mysterious. "But it's all in the book of Acts," they said, and we found they were right. Thumbing through the book of Acts we discovered several places where speaking in tongues was mentioned.

To learn more we slipped into one of their churches

on a Sunday night. We felt it wise to view the proceedings from the pew closest to the door. That way, if things got unruly we could be the first to leave.

The service was fascinating. It began with some of the most enthusiastic hymn-singing we had ever heard, and half-way through the first hymn the people began to clap their hands. We had an urge to edge for the door but within minutes our inhibitions melted away and we felt almost at home in the informal service. At our own church, with its carpeted floors and cushioned pews, such enthusiasm would have seemed out of place. But in that simple sanctuary, with its bare floors and bench-like pews, it was as natural as the plain-mannered people who made up the congregation.

After the song service there were personal testimonies and requests for prayer. Some of the testimonies sounded a bit time-worn and well-rehearsed but others, less glib, were most convincing. Many of the prayer requests were in behalf of people not present.

"Brother Jenkins asks to be remembered tonight for his back. It's been ailing him all week and he hasn't been able to work."

"Sister Molly and sister Bertha asked us to pray for their pa. Doctor says he can't last much longer and they're praying he'll find the Lord before it's too late."

Then the congregation entered into a period of corporate prayer. Although startled at first by the sudden burst of sound, we found the prayer time exhilarating. The praying voices rose and fell in mixed chorus with a kind of sing-song, chanting quality. Most were praying in English, but a few were praying in foreign-sounding languages we later discovered were "unknown tongues". After several minutes, as if by signal, the chorus of voices dwindled away and the minister rose to speak.

As far as he was concerned, the church really didn't need a pulpit. He walked as much as he talked. Striding back and forth across the platform, he preached a simple, vigorous kind of Christianity which demanded obedience to God's word and holiness from God's people. The serv-

23

ice ended with an altar call, not only for those seeking salvation, but for those seeking the baptism in the Holy Spirit as well.

We didn't quite have the nerve to go to the altar that night, but on subsequent visits to pentecostal services we did. Yet, as it turned out, our trips to the pentecostal altar proved singularly unfruitful. I remember one such venture in particular. It was the time we drove to Oklahoma City with friends to attend a large tent meeting.

During the service a woman came forward for prayer with a large unsightly goiter bulging from her neck. The evangelist placed his hand on the goiter and, supported by the believing prayers of thousands present in the tent, called on God for the woman's healing "in the mighty name of Jesus." *The goiter instantly disappeared.* A great roar of praise to God filled the tent. It was an electrifying experience which made the hair on the back of my neck stand up. The very air around us seemed to crackle, as if charged with power.

Deeply stirred by this demonstration of the healing power of God, we responded to a call for those who needed prayer for baptism in the Holy Spirit. Along with dozens of others, we were ushered into a smaller tent nearby where we knelt on the sawdust floor. Noisy and enthusiastic helpers gathered around to "pray us through". Out of the corner of my eye I noticed an elderly man who preceded us into the tent raise his hands and begin praising God in unknown tongues almost immediately. It seemed so simple for him—but it wasn't that simple for us.

So many hands were laid on my head and shoulders that I sagged under the weight. Over the din created by some who were already loudly beseeching heaven in our behalf, we began to receive all kinds of instructions.

"Just speak right out and praise God, brother!" one yelled.

"Shout 'Hallelujah!' brother," another advised. "You can't feel the Spirit unless you shout 'Hallelujah!' "

"Hold on, brother," encouraged a third.

"Let go, brother, let go!" counselled a fourth.

In addition we were told to raise our hands, to close our eyes, to take a deep breath and shout "Glory! Glory!" Also to stop praying in English and to yield and tarry. But all I could really pray for was to be left alone so we could retire from that hectic place as soon as a decent opportunity afforded itself.

"How in the world did we ever get mixed up in this?" I wondered.

Those praying with us, however, were kind and in no way critical of our stunned immobility. When we finally began to excuse ourselves and back out of the tent, they encouraged us to keep "seeking". They were right, of course. But the confusion during the time of prayer had been more than enough to block any receptivity to the Holy Spirit we may have carried with us into the tent. We had not yet discovered an important truth—namely, that the power of God was present not *because* of the noise but *in spite* of it.

But regardless of certain misgivings we were determined to continue our search for the power others had received and which the Scriptures so clearly promised. "You shall receive power when the Holy Spirit has come upon you . . ." [1] Jesus had said. Nothing could be much plainer than that.

"But can't we search for it someplace not quite so noisy?" Alice asked. I agreed it sounded like a good idea.

1. Acts 1:8

CHAPTER THREE

Not Everyone Believes

AFTER ONLY A FEW WEEKS into our search for spiritual power the disturbing realization of what "seek ye *first* the kingdom" really means began to dawn upon us. We discovered that it meant finding and following the will of God as our primary responsibility in life. Personal plans and ambitions must take a back seat. Therefore, we laid aside our hopes for a career in commercial art and began asking, "Lord, what would you have us do? Where would you have us go?"

Within a few weeks we found ourselves enrolled at the Koinonia Foundation of Baltimore, Maryland, an inter-denominational center given over to the spiritual training of Christian laymen.[1]

We had come to know about Koinonia through a small prayer group in our church. Although this group had been meeting for over two years, we'd never heard of it until a week after Dorothy's healing. Because we weren't ready, I suppose. That prayer group introduced us to a whole new world. We found that right there in our town a host of people, like ourselves, were in search of the dynamic power of God. We discovered the books of modern devotional writers like Frank Laubach, Glenn Clark, Agnes Sanford, Rufus Moseley and E. Stanley

1. After a period of spiritual and cultural training, many Koinonia-trained personnel accept assignments overseas with industry or government. A Christian forerunner of the Peace Corps, Koinonia has trained and helped place hundreds of dedicated Christians in places of great need around the world.

Jones. Also we began attending meetings where people gathered to experiment in faith and prayer.

One of Koinonia's early presidents was Dr. Frank Laubach, the world-renowned missionary and literacy expert. Laubach's books on prayer made a deep impression on us and we secretly entertained the hope that the way would open for us to join his literacy work. However, after nine months at Koinonia, we instead felt led to return to college and prepare for the preaching ministry. Dr. Albert Day, prominent Methodist minister and author, then pastor of the historic Mt. Vernon Place Methodist Church in Baltimore and member of the teaching staff of Koinonia, encouraged us in our decision.

"I know you would like to serve abroad," he told us, "but remember this: the church in America is in grave need of ministers who have first-hand experience in prayer and who are not afraid to witness to the miraculous power of God."

So in the summer of 1951 we left Koinonia to enter Bible College. The minister of our home church in Texas, Dr. George R. Davis (who later became minister of the National City Christian Church in Washington, D.C. and pastor to President Lyndon B. Johnson) had followed our spiritual quest with sympathetic interest. But when we told him of our plans to enter Bible College at Phillips University in Enid, Oklahoma, his own alma mater, he replied, "I'm not sure you will find what you're looking for in any Bible college. However, I'll help you all I can." And help he did, for it was through his influence that we received generous financial assistance from the church during our years of ministerial training.

It did not take long to discover the reason for Dr. Davis' rather puzzling remark. Our liberal colleges and seminaries place so much emphasis on the critical approach to Christianity that they often run roughshod over a student's tender faith in Jesus Christ. The mortality rate ministerial students is disturbingly high. Finding it impossible to keep, or nurture, the reality of his Christian experience in such a cold atmosphere, many a disillusioned student either switches to another field of study or leaves college altogether. Either way the loss to the Christian ministry is substantial.

Coming out of the prayerful environment of Koinonia Foundation and fresh from the influence of teachers like Frank Laubach and Dr. Albert Day, I had difficulty in becoming adjusted to the more sophisticated approach to the Christian faith which characterized Bible College. And while my years at Phillips University provided essential training and discipline in preparation for the preaching ministry, in one major area of the Christian life I remained at loggerheads with most of my professors. I simply could not reconcile their deep devotion and commitment to Christ, their obvious intellectual honesty and integrity, with their rejection of the supernatural elements in the Christian faith.

Why should those who love Jesus Christ want to strip Him of His power, I wondered? Yet even those professors who believed the New Testament account of miracles carefully explained to their students that such supernatural acts of the Holy Spirit ended at the close of the first century.

"The miracle-working power of the Holy Spirit ceased with the death of the Apostles and the ones on whom they laid their hands. Miracles were a temporary phenomenon used by God to help get the Church started. Once the Church was established, the supernatural gifts disappeared." Such ran the argument with which claims for modern miracles were dismissed. I remember coming away from a class in New Testament one day deeply dismayed over the professor's concluding remarks. In a neat display of verbal gymnastics he encouraged us to pray while at the same time denying the possibility of tangible answers to our prayers.

Another professor spoke convincingly against what he called the "healing sects" calling them "a blight on the face of Christianity". When I suggested there seemed to be Scriptural grounds for establishing such a ministry, he retorted, "The Scriptures you quote about the power of prayer were meant only for the Apostles, and anyone believing them today is either ignorant or incredibly naive." I assumed he felt I filled both qualifications quite well.

But while Phillips University—like all liberal Christian colleges and seminaries—had its share of intellectual skeptics, still it was marked by a certain warm, devotional spirit, fostered in no little part by the leadership of its president, Dr. Eugene S. Briggs, and his lovely wife. We were grateful for the friendship of the Briggs, who were sympathetic with our spiritual quest. The time was to come when their trust and confidence in us would be a welcome haven in a storm of controversy.

Fully convinced of the reality of God's power by experiences in his own life, Dr. Briggs periodically invited men of prayer to come and speak at chapel services. One year Dr. Roland Brown, a Baptist minister with a striking ministry in the field of spiritual healing, came on campus as speaker for Religious Emphasis Week. To the surprise of students and professors alike, he spoke boldly of the power of God to heal, illustrating his sermons with miraculous experiences drawn from his own ministry.

Copies of a book describing Pastor Brown's ministry were available at the campus book store. One critical professor brought a copy to his class one morning and held it up before his students.

"See this book?" his voice was shaking in anger. "This is the biggest joke book ever written!" Then, slamming the book down on his desk, he ripped into Brown's ministry, depicting it as one appealing only to dupes and simpletons.

Other guest speakers seemed to agree with Pastor Brown's critic. One prominent homiletics professor from a leading Eastern seminary interrupted his guest lecture with a stern warning to the student ministers that unless they learned to sidestep or ignore them, they would be pestered to death by little old ladies in their congregations who would always be asking, "Preacher, will prayer help?"

Although the majority of my text books and lectures gave little place to prayer, except for its psychological benefits, by contrast our college library was loaded with devotional literature clearly testifying to its actual power. Therefore, I tried to balance my required reading in the fields of theology and Biblical criticism with generous portions of devotional reading which warmed the heart and lifted the spirit.

Another point of restlessness were classes on church administrative techniques. These seemed aimed primarily to teach us how to achieve statistical results while ignoring spiritual motivation. Successful ministers from large nearby churches would occasionally be invited to lecture on such matters. I recall one who addressed a class of mine. A tall, stately figure of a man with wavy, silver hair and solemn visage, he looked every inch the successful executive. With a deep, assured voice he announced to the class his intention to share the crowning achievement of his fifteen years in the influential church he pastored.

His testimony was short and simple. It concerned his finesse in the art of fund-raising which, over a period of years, had enabled him to raise the level of giving in his two-thousand member church by approximately ten cents per week per member. "The thrilling result of that achievement," he concluded in a voice booming like an Old Testament prophet, "was a half-million dollar program to restore the historic building of our great church —and we did it *practically painlessly*." His voice dropped to a dramatic stage whisper on the last two words.

I remarked to my professor at the close of the class that if "practically painless fund-raising" was what was meant by success in the ministry, I wasn't sure I wanted to succeed.

Such lectures not only left the power of the Holy Spirit safely embalmed in history, but also implied that no modern Christian need seek the transforming power of God. Spiritual revival is only an historic phenomenon to be analyzed, never a present reality to be experienced, and the Church an institution rich in tradition and significantly linked to a great past, but largely impervious to any supernatural moving of the Holy Spirit in our day. Such a Church was a far cry from the one I sought to serve.

Although applying myself diligently to study and eventually finishing seminary in the top quarter of my class, I never could be reconciled to what I felt was a serious flaw in the college's ministerial training program. The emphasis on rationalistic explorations in the fields of theology and Biblical criticism and the development of professional ministerial techniques was clearly out of balance with the obvious under-emphasis on spiritual disciplines. My years in the pastorate since graduation have only strengthened the conviction that our Christian colleges and seminaries need a much deeper approach to their task of training ministers. God grant that the day may come when they will feel called to instill a vital, flaming faith in the hearts of their students which will more than match the scholastic and administrative skills they now impart so effectively.

CHAPTER FOUR

Elder Sammytinger's Chocolate Pie

HOLDING AN IMPORTANT PLACE in the life of most any Bible college or seminary is the carefully developed and maintained program of student pastorates. The only way the student minister learns to preach is by the experience of preaching. Phillips University supplied student ministers for well over a hundred Christian churches within a two-hundred mile radius of the campus. While a few students who preached close to the seminary lived on the field and commuted to classes, most lived in Enid and drove to their churches for the week-end.

Every Friday afternoon saw a mass exodus from the campus, as scores of young ministers climbed into cars and struck off in all directions to render youthful, optimistic Christian service across Oklahoma, Kansas and even to border areas of Missouri and Texas. A few served as youth directors or associate ministers in the larger city churches, but most pastored small congregations of one hundred members or less. The quality of preaching may have left something to be desired, but the program provided the students with preaching and pastoral experience and made it possible for a large number of small churches to have a regular ministry which otherwise would have been unable to afford a resident pastor.

When a ministerial student completed most of his undergraduate study he became eligible for a student preaching point. In the spring of my junior year I reached this stage and filled out an application. One day, soon after, the director of field service called me into his office.

"Don, I see you're eligible to serve a church now.

Well, a church in eastern Kansas telephoned this morning. Their student minister has found a church closer to Enid and they want someone to preach for them this week-end."

I jumped at the chance and rushed home to tell Alice. "Honey, I'm preaching this Sunday!" Alice looked up from her ironing. "That's nice," she said. "Where?"

In my excitement I had forgotten the name of the place. All I could remember was that it was someplace in Kansas. Thrusting my hand in my pocket I retrieved a crumpled slip of paper the director of field service had handed me.

"It's a place called Edna, Kansas. Near Coffeyville."

"Where's Coffeyville?"

I hadn't the foggiest notion, so we dug out a tattered road atlas to look. After a brief search we located Coffeyville, then Edna.

"Looks like it's a long way from here," Alice mused.

I added up the miles. "Two hundred and sixty miles, one way," I said lamely. "No wonder their minister wanted a church closer to Enid." But the appointment was for only one Sunday, and every young preacher has to start somewhere.

To make the long drive we left early Sunday morning while it was still dark. We arrived in plenty of time, but "first-sermon jitters" had taken hold of me and I was all full of flutters. I spent the minutes before the service checking hymn numbers an the order of worship with the pianist and one of the elders—trying not to look nervous. We had been told that both Edna and the church were small. That was an understatement. Edna was not really a town, just an intersection of roads with a service station and general store. And the Elm Christian Church had what is generously referred to as a "modest" congregation. Given good weather and the right time of year Sunday attendance, percentage-wise, was excellent. Bad weather or harvest season, we were told, cut the crowd considerably. The Sunday we were there it was good weather and a full two weeks before the beginning of

33

harvest, so the congregation turned out full strength. Including all the children there were thirty-two people present. I know because I counted them. Twice.

I announced the opening hymn and the service began to move forward with a kind of hesitant efficiency. All too soon it was time for my sermon. My text was the story of the Rich Young Ruler—"Good Master, what shall I do to inherit eternal life?"—but I confess my primary concern was not so much with spiritual profundity. There was the more pressing problem of filling the allotted sermon time with coherent speech before either my voice or my knees gave out. The service was a success only in that I was able to get through the worship hour without committing some glaring error. As I walked up the aisle to the back of the church to pronounce the benediction, I wiped my brow with my handkerchief and silently thanked the Lord for getting me through the service.

Afterward we were invited to the home of one of the elders of the church for Sunday dinner, and I remember our visit to Edna more for the lesson I learned in that home than for it being my initial preaching endeavor. We gathered around a table laden with the bounty common to midwestern farm folk. There were heaping platters of fried chicken, white mountains of mashed potatoes, cream gravy, bowls of cooked vegetables, crisp green salads and spicy pickles, hot biscuits with melted butter and homemade peach preserves. I responded with sincerity when asked to "return thanks". After the prayer Mrs. Sammytinger, our hostess, left the table and returned carrying a plate with a huge slab of chocolate pie which she placed in front of her husband.

"Pa doesn't like to end his meals on anything sweet," she explained, "so he has his dessert first. You folks just go ahead and help yourselves to the chicken." So while we ate fried chicken, Elder Sammytinger ate chocolate pie. Later, while we ate chocolate pie, he ate fried chicken. Although I studiously avoided any comment, Elder Sammytinger noted my surprise and after dinner

34

shared with me the philosophy behind the reversal of menu.

"Now preacher, I'll agree that in the Old Testament the Lord has quite a bit to say about what's fit to eat and what isn't. But I don't recall Him ever saying what order we had to eat it in, do you? I don't think He minds if my eating habits differ from yours or the other fellow's. The way I figure it, if it satisfies me, it satisfies Him."

I smiled and quoted for him Emerson's famous statement, "He who would be a man must be a nonconformist." Elder Sammytinger laughed, slapped his knee and said, "Well, I guess that means I qualify."

Many times since then I have recalled the incident of Elder Sammytinger's chocolate pie. It has helped me refrain from hasty criticism of others, as well as helping me be true to myself even when it meant "being different". There is good common sense in refusing to be bound by customs which have no true worth in themselves and are not of our making or to our liking. I had preached a sermon from the pulpit that day, but Elder Sammytinger preached a better one at the dinner table.

CHAPTER FIVE

The Lord Will Provide—Even Spare Parts

MY FIRST REGULAR STUDENT PASTORATE was in Burkburnett, Texas, which although not quite so far as Edna, Kansas, was still a *weary* 210 miles from school. Another student preaching in a nearby town rode with me. Leaving for Burkburnett after Friday classes were over I would drop Charles off at Lawton, Oklahoma, and pick him up on the return trip Sunday night.

Looking back I marvel at the Divine protection extended to the 140 young ministers like ourselves who drove thousands of miles in all kinds of weather at all hours of the day and night to render our Christian service. Guardian angels whom the Lord must surely have appointed to keep watch over that perambulating flock of preachers worked overtime, for I do not recall a single student minister being involved in a serious automobile accident during my years on campus. There were plenty of narrow escapes—but more about that later.

Our Friday afternoon trips to the church were usually pleasant and uneventful, but that return trip Sunday night was something else. After a long week-end which included pastoral visitation, teaching Sunday school and preaching both morning and evening services, we would crawl into the car and head back for Enid, bone-tired even before the trip began. Fighting weariness and staving off the treacherous fingers of sleep which constantly tugged at our eyelids, we would arrive back in Enid in the infant hours of the morning to snatch a few hours' sleep before meeting a 9:00 a.m. class.

Charles and I resorted to all kinds of measures in our

battle to stay awake. We would rehash our sermons, sing hymns, stop for coffee and cokes, slap one another on the back, lean out the window and shout at the wind and then start the whole cycle over again. When nothing worked we would finally give in, pull off the road and sleep; but this meant arriving in Enid stiff-necked and late for class.

The most treacherous thing about those midnight rides, we discovered, was the danger of going to sleep with your eyes open. Many a time I sat up with a start after dozing open-eyed for several seconds while the car drifted until two wheels were off the pavement. We found ourselves praying there would be oncoming traffic to break the hypnotic effect of miles of straight, empty highway. There were times when we slowed down or swerved to miss obstacles which weren't really there.

One Monday a student came to class claiming he had actually seen three camels crossing the highway the night before. We couldn't resist asking him if they had been carrying the three wise men. Two other young ministers were returning across the empty miles of Oklahoma's western plains late one Sunday night, taking turns at the wheel. All at once the student asleep in back awoke, realizing the car had stopped. He sat up and looked around only to discover they were miles from anywhere. No town, no traffic, no highway intersection, no stop light, nothing. His partner was sitting behind the wheel staring down the empty highway. The engine was idling. "Why'dja stop?" came the sleepy question. Still staring straight ahead, the driver replied slowly, "I'm waiting for the train to pass." Wide-awake and goggle-eyed, the other student heaved himself into the front seat. "Move over and let me drive! You need sleep!"

Like most student ministers we lived on next-to-nothing plus a little faith. Each week-end saw Charles and me with just enough cash to get by until we received our pay from our churches on Sunday night. Our combined financial resources on one particular Friday afternoon totaled slightly over four dollars. I remember it well, for there haven't been many Friday afternoons when I witnessed a miracle.

Charles and I often engaged in vigorous theological discussions while traveling together. A brilliant and dedicated student, Charles tended to view with tolerant skepticism my more simple approach to the Christian faith and my firm belief in the power of prayer and the gifts of the Holy Spirit. In spite of our differences, however, we were good friends.

Our route led down U.S. Highway 81—at that time a major traffic artery between Wichita, Kansas, and Dallas, Texas. About two hours out of Enid the old engine of the 1948 Chevrolet I was driving suddenly quit without so much as a gasp. We rolled to the side of the highway and stopped. A brief look under the hood showed something drastically wrong with the distributor; it was cocked at a crazy angle and the cap had been knocked loose. There we stood, two dejected, nearly-broke, would-be ministers of the gospel, miles from the nearest town, gloomily reciting to each other various plans of action, any one of which would cost money—lots of money!

I could catch a ride to the nearest town, wire a relative for funds to hire a tow truck to come and pick up the car. But even thinking of the cost of such a maneuver made me wince. Or, we could leave the car and hitch-hike to our churches. I could plead my case before the church treasurer and ask for an advance on my salary, then return for the car. But again I shuddered to contemplate the cost, and who knew what vandalism the car might suffer left untended beside the busy highway.

I leaned against the fender and gazed morosely at the steady stream of traffic flowing past. Almost without realizing it I found myself pouring out our predicament in silent prayer to God. Knowing how Charles felt, I didn't have the nerve to ask him to pray with me. "We're in a fine fix, Lord," I fumed. "If there was ever a time we could use a little help from you, it's now!" I recalled old Jehoshaphat's lament to the Lord, "We do not know what to do, but our eyes are upon Thee."[1]

That was us, all right. *Helpless!* As the sun set and it began to grow dark my concern increased. Alice had stayed at the parsonage during the week and would soon be expecting me. I sighed and kicked one of the tires with my toe. "Darned old wreck!" There's nothing more useless than an automobile you know won't run.

A half hour of helpless waiting had passed when a car pulled out of the line of traffic and stopped. It was a young couple with a baby between them on the front seat. The driver poked his head out of the window.

"Got troubles?"

"Our distributor's haywire," I remarked glumly.

"Mind if I take a look?"

"Don't think it'll do any good. We need a new distributor."

"Let me take a look anyway. You got a flashlight or any tools?"

"No."

"Well, never mind. I got a trunk full of tools and we'll use my flashlight." Then, as I held the light, with a few deft turns of a wrench he removed the distributor. It was easy to see he was an automobile mechanic. Hefting the troublesome part in his hand he confirmed our suspicion.

"You're right. It's shot. Shaft's froze up solid. You'll need another distributor."

I thanked him for his trouble and suggested the best thing might be for us to catch a ride with him to the next town and send back for the car. I hated to admit our precarious financial status.

"Maybe you could swap this distributor for another one and save a little money," he ventured, ignoring my suggestion. With a shrug I then admitted our predicament. "We only have about four dollars between us. That won't buy much of a distributor."

1. II Chronicles 20:12

Still toying with the part in his hands he said, "Maybe I can get you another distributor for free."

"For free?" we chorused. A slight shiver tingled up my spine and some inner witness signaled the Holy Spirit was at work. I waited expectantly to see what would happen next.

"Hop in the car," the mechanic said. "We just need to go down the road a ways to get it." Without another word we crawled in the back seat of his car. I was surprised when he turned the car around and headed down the highway in the opposite direction. After a few miles we turned onto a dirt road and soon pulled up next to a farm house.

"My in-laws live here," our benefactor explained, and turning to his wife he said, "Honey, take the baby on into the house and send your brother out here to help me." As his wife entered the house he swung the car around. The headlights probed through the farmyard past various pieces of worn-out machinery to reveal the rusting remains of an old 1942 Chevrolet, minus wheels and one door. We followed him over to the metal ruin and watched as he shone the flashlight on the remains of the engine. With a grunt of satisfaction he bent over and quickly removed the distributor, then holding it up to the light, compared it with the one taken from our car.

"I thought so. They didn't change 'em a bit. This old '42's the same as your '48. He handed the distributor to his young brother-in-law. "Here, Jimmy, put a little gasoline in a bucket and wash this thing off."

Minutes later we were back in his car returning to the highway. "Sorry to put you to all this trouble," I began to apologize.

"S'all right," he replied. "You see, I work in a garage over in Oklahoma City and the wife and me, we were just on the way to her folks' house for the weekend. I saw you standing by your car and wanted to stop but my wife, she says, 'Oh, let's don't! You don't know what kind of men they are.' She thought you might be

40

crooks or something. So we drove on. But somehow it kept nagging at me that we shoulda stopped. Finally, as we turned off to go to her pa's place, I said, 'Honey, I think we shoulda helped those men.' Well, you coulda knocked me over with a feather when she says, 'All right. If you feel that way about it, *then turn around and go back.*' So I did."

We arrived back at our car and in a few minutes he installed the distributor, adjusted the timing and gave me the nod. "Try her now." I stepped on the starter and the old car roared into life. Resisting our efforts to give him our last four dollars he said, "Nossir! Can't take money for helping out folks who need it. If things'd been reversed you'da done the same for me." Then he was gone.

I sat gratefully behind the wheel for a moment until Charles spoke impatiently. "Let's get going. What are you waiting for?"

"I was just thanking God for getting us out of that mess."

Charles laughed. "Oh, come on now, how can you be sure it was God? Me, I'm just thankful the world has a few good men left in it, like that one."

"You mean you don't think it was the Lord's doing?"

Charles remained dubious, so I recounted the amazing list of things that had happened. Of the hundreds of cars which passed us on the highway, only one stopped, and that one carried a mechanic who not only had the knowledge, but the flashlight, the tools, the willingness to help, plus a father-in-law with a farmyard only a few miles away where the rusty carcass of a twelve-year-old car contained the very part we needed.

"It could have been just the long arm of coincidence," Charles insisted doubtfully. The list had shaken him a bit.

"Maybe so," I said. "But tell me this one last thing. After they had already passed us by and had traveled

41

three miles down the road, *Who* made the wife change her mind and tell her husband to turn around and come back to help us?"

Charles grinned sheepishly and said nothing. But he knew well enough *Who*.

And so did I.

CHAPTER SIX

Sermons and Storms and Miracles

NOT LONG AFTER THE INCIDENT involving the distributor I left the small church at Burkburnett to begin a week-end ministry at the Christian Church in Howard, Kansas, a small county-seat town about 80 miles east of Wichita. True to my convictions I immediately began to preach about the power of God to answer our prayers and to heal and transform our lives. People in that conservative, rural congregation gave me a polite hearing but were not particularly receptive. They had endured a succession of student ministers, and I suspect years of listening to young, green preachers preaching young, green sermons had thoroughly conditioned them against any but the most cautious response to the current student's enthusiasms.

The classrooms in the church basement were given over to the children's Sunday school, making it necessary for the two adult classes to meet simultaneously in the small sanctuary, one up front near the pulpit, the other back by the windows. For the newcomer it sounded like bedlam as the teachers' voices bounced off the walls and collided in mid-sanctuary. It took me several weeks to learn how to tune one out and tune in the other.

The class I had been invited to attend—not teach, mind you, just attend—was taught by the chairman of the church board who quickly made it plain he did not share my convictions about the current availability of God's miracle-working power. Any Sunday he disagreed with something in my sermon, the following week the

Sunday school lesson would include his opinion on the subject.

One Sunday I preached on miracles and the following week, true to form, he broached the subject during his lesson. Addressing the whole class but looking straight at me he said, "Now some people believe miracles like those Jesus and the disciples performed still happen, but most *intelligent* people know the age of miracles is past."

Although obviously excluded from the intelligentsia, I smiled at him anyway and offered no defense of my position. I was content to bide my time and wait for the Holy Spirit to move.

The week-end trips to Howard were far less strenuous than those to my former church. Howard was closer to school. Also, by then I was enrolled in the graduate seminary which scheduled no Monday classes, so the need for late Sunday night driving had ended.

Our old Chevrolet performed admirably for many months with its miracle distributor, but finally normal wear made it necessary to secure another car. In a way we were reluctant to part with it, for it was a constant reminder to us of the providence of God. But in the small Studebaker sedan, which became our next car, we were soon to be reminded in even more dramatic fashion of God's protecting hand over our lives.

It was a wintry Monday afternoon and we were returning to Enid from our week-end at Howard. For an hour we had driven with extra care since a snowstorm Sunday night had left stretches of icy pavement and places where snow had drifted deep across the highway. But once beyond the path of the storm we found the road clear and dry and with relief I resumed normal speed as we ticked off the miles toward home.

We were approaching a small town near the Kansas-Oklahoma border when it happened. Bearing down on a sharp S-curve which marked the highway's approach to the town, the terrifying realization hit me that the highway beneath our wheels had filmed over with a thin, in-

44

visible sheath of ice. Cautiously I touched the brake pedal only to lift my foot instantly as the rear of the car swung ominously in the beginning of a skid.

"Ice!" I gasped. "We'll never make that curve!" Instinctively I breathed a desperate prayer, "Oh Lord, help us!"

In such emergencies things happen in a fraction of a second which later take long minutes to describe. Since braking was impossible and any effort to make the turn at such high speed would result in the car flipping over the embankment, we had only one choice and that was to leave the road.

"Hang on, Alice," I yelled as the road began to curve out from under us. I gripped the wheel as firmly as I could in an effort to maintain some measure of control over the car, as we left the pavement and pitched over the embankment.

The point at which we left the road was marked by a narrow track of dirt ruts which led down the embankment to an old fence some hundred yards away. We sailed a number of feet through the air and slammed into those ruts as the car hit the ground. I jammed on the brakes and tried in vain to hold the car straight as it tore along the rough ground, then swerved out of the ruts to plow into a dense thicket of wild plum bushes. Losing speed as we burst out of the thicket, the car bounced back across the ruts into high weeds on the other side. I pumped the brakes furiously as I saw fence posts looming dead ahead. The car swerved crazily one more time and we skidded to a stop almost touching the fence. After a moment of stunned silence I turned to Alice.

"Are you all right?"

She nodded mutely, as tears of relief began streaming down her cheeks. I opened the door and walked shaky-legged around the car. Except for some paint scratches there was no damage. I looked back past the swath we had cut through the plum thicket to the highway and what I saw made me shakier still. The embankment was high and deadly steep all along the curve. Only at the exact spot where we left the road, where earth had been filled in to build the narrow rutted path we had struck, could a car have left the road without overturning. Had we left the highway an instant sooner or an instant later the results would have been disastrous.

"For He will give His angels charge over you to guard you in all your ways." I found myself softly quoting the familiar words of the ninety-first Psalm.

"What did you say?" Alice called through the car window.

"Nothing," I replied, and turning the car around we gingerly nosed our way back up onto the highway and turned again for home.

* * * *

No matter where you live you have to put up with the weather, and anyone living in the southwestern part of the United States is aware of an annual peril—the tornado season. Each year, in the late spring and early summer, weather conditions frequently combine to spawn those devilish storms.

One spring night, during that year I was preaching in Howard, a huge funnel dipped out of a storm-filled sky to twist its tortuous way across the countryside. Blackwell, Oklahoma, about fifty miles from Enid, lay sleeping in its path and was hit almost before the sirens sounded warning. Striking the southeast corner of that peaceful town of 20,000 souls, the twister ground out its deadly path, leaving scores dead, hundreds injured and millions of dollars in property damage. The funnel lifted as it left the stricken town and moved relentlessly to the northeast, across the Kansas border, before dipping with evil capriciousness once more and raging into the tiny community of Udall, Kansas, devouring it completely. Every home and building in the village was destroyed and less than a dozen people out of the community of almost one hundred survived.

My route to Howard lay through Blackwell. Two

days after the storm I passed through on my way to the church. The business district had been largely untouched but the highway out of town, which had once led through a district marked by stately trees and Blackwell's finest old homes, was now merely a cleared strip of pavement between rows of fallen bricks and splintered rubble. It was as if some massive grinder had chewed a mile-wide corner off the town. Grim-faced patrols with civil-defense arm bands motioned me to keep moving as in my mind I began to frame the outline of a sermon on natural evil and the Christian faith. The message I had intended to preach on Sunday was rendered totally irrelevant by what I had seen.

Stopping at a town some miles from Howard to visit a parishioner recovering from surgery, I entered the small hospital to find the corridors crowded with beds containing injured survivors of the storm. Sharing the room with my parishioner was one of the few Udall survivors, an elderly widow who looked as if someone had taken a club and beaten her. She told me her story.

She had been alone in her two-story frame house watching television. Outside it was pouring rain. The TV program had just been interrupted with a weather bulletin warning that a funnel had been sighted near the Kansas border and advising people in the area to take cover in storm cellars and basements.

"The idea never entered my mind that the twister might be coming toward us," she shook her bandaged head sadly. "Then, above the rain I heard an awful sound—like a train a'comin', it was—only much louder. Besides, I knew Udall didn't even have a railroad. Then it happened . . ." She shuddered and closed her eyes against the memory.

Before she could get out of her chair the roar became deafening and the house began to shake and tremble. The lights went out and the sound of creaking nails as the timbers in the house began to wrench apart was like a thousand screams. Suddenly the house exploded all around her and the next thing she knew she

47

was lying flat on her back in the open air, being pelted by the rain, apparently free from serious injury. But the twister howled its way into the distance only to be followed by a savage hailstorm pounding along in its wake. Helpless amid the wreckage the dear old lady had taken a brutal beating from the hail. The bombardment of those icy missiles, some as large as baseballs, had left her suffering multiple bruises, fractured ribs and severe cuts around the face and head. But more terrifying than either the twister or the hail had been the awful darkness and silence which followed. It was almost two hours after the storm before she saw the first lights and heard the first voices of those coming to her aid.

In my sermon on Sunday I tried to view the tragedy in relation to the will of God for our lives. Even to this day I am astonished at the number of Christians who so quickly and glibly rationalize such tragedy with the statement, "It must have been God's will." That morning I shared as simply as I could my conviction that God's will for us is *good*, and that disaster, either man-made or natural, is certainly not what He desires for us.

While completely satisfactory answers to the problem may elude us, there is indication in Scripture that, as the power of God triumphs over sin and moral evil, the disharmonies and conflicts within the natural order of things may disappear as well. Not only did Jesus have power over storms, but Paul, in his Roman letter, indicates a relationship between nature and the evil in man. He says that the creation itself is in bondage, waiting "for the revealing of the sons of God."[1]

I related an incident of some years earlier in which friends of ours in Oklahoma City received word of strange predictive prophecy coming from praying friends in Waco, Texas. The prophecies foretold how the city of Waco was in danger of violent destruction and urged earnest prayer that the city might be spared. The unusual nature of the prophecies—so similar to some in the Old Testament—had led these Christians in Waco to

1. Romans 8:18-23

48

contact their Oklahoma City friends for additional prayer help. A few days later the warnings of disaster were fulfilled when a destructive tornado twisted through the heart of the city, taking a very heavy toll in human life and destroying millions of dollars worth of property.[2]

After the sermon one of the church deacons paused at the door.

"Then you don't believe it was God's will for those people to be killed in the storm?"

"Absolutely not!"

"But how can you be sure? Folks around here are all saying it was God's doing—that He was punishing those people for their wickedness. They say it *was* the will of God and we just have to accept it."

"Well, suppose the twister had headed for your farm, threatening your family," I countered. "As a Christian would you have calmly awaited its approach saying, 'The Lord gives and the Lord takes away, blessed be the name of the Lord,' or would you have made a beeline for the storm cellar?"

The deacon smiled. "I'da run like crazy for the cellar!"

"Exactly!" I said. "And if I'd been there I would have been right behind you. And I don't think either one of us would have been running from the will of God." The argument might not have been profound, but it was effective at the time.

Less than one week later Howard itself was barely spared the fate of Udall. About sundown the following Friday a twister came churning up the fields southwest of town, Howard directly in its path. Suddenly, the funnel lifted and roared across town about treetop height, twisting and splintering the topmost branches of the trees, uprooting some and felling others, ripping off shingles and shattering windows and momentarily reducing much of the population to a state of near panic

2. An article in *Christian Life Magazine*, July 1964, p. 26, describes the incident.

since visions of Blackwell and Udall were still fresh in mind.

"How can you explain it?" I was asked the following Sunday. "Why was Howard spared when Blackwell and Udall were not?" I confessed I had no pat answer.

"Let's just be grateful the town was spared," I said. I couldn't help noting the attendance at church that day was much larger than usual.

*   *   *   *

A few weeks later we arrived at the parsonage for the week-end and found George, the church clerk who lived next door, out working in his yard. He saw us drive in and as he came toward us I could tell by the way he walked he was excited about something.

"Hey, Don, do you remember one Sunday when you preached on spiritual healing and mentioned that fellow, Oral Roberts?"

"I surely do," I smiled. As I recalled, the sermon had gone over like a lead balloon. My insistence that we should not hesitate to pray for miracles of healing had met with a cool response.

"Well, I thought you went off the deep end in that sermon," George continued with a frankness characteristic of him. "But last week my wife and I went to visit her parents over in Missouri. Roberts' program came on TV one night while we were there, and they wanted us to watch it with them. I doubt if I'da stayed in the room to watch if you hadn't mentioned him in that sermon. But I'll have to admit it—he sure can preach!

"Then we watched the healing service. I wasn't impressed until he prayed for a little six-year-old boy. You could tell from the youngster's expression that he *felt* something! Walked off the stage without his crutches, too."

I smiled and started into the parsonage with our suitcases. George followed me, still talking.

"I tell you that really got to me! I felt like crying— can you imagine? Then, after the healing service, this guy Roberts prayed for those of us watching on TV. Now mind you, the whole program was taped—a recording several weeks old. But when that man prayed, I tell you, Don, *Something* came right into the living room where we sat. We all felt it! It actually frightened me! But that's not all. My mother-in-law had been suffering for weeks with some kind of weird facial paralysis—I forget what the doctor called it—but he said there wasn't much he could do for it."

"Bell's palsy?" I offered.

"Yes, that's what he called it," George nodded. "Anyway, when Oral Roberts prayed, her paralysis instantly disappeared. I was so shook up by what happened I didn't know what to do. I had never felt the power of God before, and believe me, it's awesome."

I went into the kitchen and took three soft drinks from the refrigerator. Opening the bottles I handed George one, and he followed me out of the house to the car where Alice was finishing the unloading.

"Here, honey." I handed her the other bottle of pop as George continued.

"Well, we came back home in time for me to go to the men's mid-week Bible study at the church. I was still so excited about the whole thing that when I got the chance I told them what happened."

George paused and shook his head ruefully, "But did I ever put my foot in it! The longer I talked the more pained they looked. Everyone got *real* quiet. I'm not sure a single man there believed my story. I felt like an idiot, and now I'm almost sorry I tried to share with them what happened."

Abruptly he started back toward his house and I thought our conversation had ended, until he turned suddenly and came striding back to where I stood. Handing me the untouched bottle of pop, he grinned sheepishly.

"You know, I've been in this church a long time, and I've watched you preachers come and go. Frankly, I've never been too impressed with any of you. And the church—well, I suppose I just took it for granted. But deep down I've always hoped there was something more to this Christianity business than I had ever experienced. Now I know there is!"

Sunday night after church, Alice and I were invited over to the board chairman's house for coffee. He was the Sunday school teacher who insisted the age of miracles had passed. After some initial polite conversation Virgil got to the point.

"Did you hear what happened to George's mother-in-law?"

"Yes, I heard."

"Well, I don't know whether to believe it or not. Ever since I was a kid I've been taught in Sunday school —and I believed it—that this kind of thing just can't happen any more. Besides, how do we know Sally's mother's paralysis wouldn't have gone away at that very moment, even if they had not been watching Oral Roberts pray? The doctors said it might go away of its own accord."

I agreed that was a possibility.

We continued the discussion for a while with Virgil firing sharp questions at me and at the same time carrying on a rather one-sided conversation with himself. It was obvious that he was trying hard to hold on to his past teaching in the face of a seeming miracle which contradicted those teachings.

Then, suddenly changing the subject, he began talking about a problem facing one of our church families. A mother, greatly concerned about her rebellious teenage daughter, was almost facing a nervous breakdown. For weeks she had been suffering from acute insomnia, and Virgil wondered what we might do to help the family.

"I'll be glad to talk with her," I offered, "but we might be able to help them even sooner by praying for them." Virgil stirred uneasily in his chair and I quickly assured him I would offer the prayer if he and his wife would join in silently. We grew quiet and I offered a brief prayer asking God to come in and manifest His love and peace in that family's situation and to grant rest to the mother. I had an inner witness that something good was happening even before the prayer ended. As we said goodbye at the door, I noticed what looked suspiciously like a tear in Virgil's eye.

Two weeks later when we arrived at the parsonage, George, the church clerk, was waiting for us.

"Remember the night you went over to Virgil's and prayed for Nell's insomnia?"

"Yes, we remember."

"Well, I don't think Virgil has the nerve to tell you what happened, but he told me and I knew you would be interested. He ran into Nell on the street a few days later and asked how she was feeling. She said she had been feeling fine ever since Sunday night, when for the first time in weeks she went to bed early. She retired about ten o'clock, slept the whole night through and has slept soundly every night since. Told Virgil she and her daughter were getting along better, too."

George laughed and concluded, "Virgil admitted to me it had been about ten o'clock when you folks prayed for Nell."

Virgil never mentioned the incident to me, but some weeks later as I sat in his Sunday school class, the question of miracles was raised again. Virgil addressed the class but caught my eye as he spoke. "Now, some people think the age of miracles is past. In fact, I used to think so myself. But most intelligent people know they still can happen when people pray and have faith." He winked at me and then continued the lesson.

CHAPTER SEVEN

Ready to Receive

ALTHOUGH THERE WERE MANY EVIDENCES of God's Spirit at work in our lives and affairs during those first years at Phillips University, the answer to our prayer for baptism in the Holy Spirit was destined to come at a location far removed from the college campus.

At the end of my junior year we returned to Koinonia Foundation in Baltimore, Maryland, to work for the summer. It was there, while attending a spiritual retreat not far from the city, that we met Harald Bredesen, a minister who now serves the First Reformed Church in Mt. Vernon, New York. Through friends we had previously heard about some of this man's remarkable experiences.

One of the most striking was the time Harald was standing in the lobby of a New York City hotel giving his Christian witness to a young Egyptian woman, the daughter of a dealer in Egyptian antiquities. Suddenly Harald began praying aloud in an unknown tongue. The young woman, an accomplished linguist, was momentarily speechless with astonishment. Then she asked Harald where he had learned ancient Arabic. She quickly wrote down about forty words in the strange dialect which Harald had used. She also observed how language scholars, even after years of study, could not speak that ancient tongue without a clumsy accent. Harald's speech, however, had been without a trace of accent.

"You sound just like an old Bedouin saying his prayers on his prayer rug," she said. When Harald read to her the account of Pentecost from his pocket Testament she was deeply moved, knowing she had witnessed the same supernatural phenomenon.

We shared with Harald our deep desire to receive the baptism in the Holy Spirit, not knowing at the time that God would use him as an instrument in helping answer our prayer.

As the summer grew to a close we began to explore the possibility of attending a "Camp Farthest Out" prayer retreat which was to be held on Star Island, one of the Isles of Shoals off the coast of Portsmouth, New Hampshire. In addition to Dr. Glenn Clark, founder of the CFO movement, the leadership was to include Rufus Moseley, whose books and personal testimony had made a deep impression on us, and Harald Bredesen. But the Star Island Camp was one of the most popular of the many CFO's held across the country and our inquiry revealed that reservations had been sold out weeks before. Neither had we any way of financing the trip. Indeed, after investigation, the whole idea seemed out of the question. But some inner prompting kept nagging at us not to give up. In fact, after much earnest prayer, we began to feel God really wanted us to go.

Like Gideon of old, we put out fleeces to test the Lord.[1] We prayed that if all the obstacles to our attending the Star Island Camp were removed and we did go, we would accept it as a sign from the Lord that during the retreat we would receive the baptism in the Holy Spirit. Committing the matter into the hands of God we stepped back and waited. In the quiet way God so often works, the obstacles which first loomed so large began to disappear.

First came word that full scholarships were available to student ministers and their wives. That meant us.

"But what good are scholarships if we have no room?" my wife asked realistically. Two days later her question was answered when we received word of a reservation cancellation which provided us with a room.

1. See Judges 6:36-40

Then our transportation problem was solved when I was asked to be the driver of a car scheduled to carry some of the Koinonia staff to Star Island.

But in spite of all these small miracles, one stubborn obstacle remained—money. We were practically down to our last dime. Even with all the help already in sight, we knew we would need some money for meals enroute and other incidental expenses.

On our arrival at Koinonia at the beginning of summer we had carefully laid aside eighty-five dollars, the amount needed to pay our way back to Enid when time came to return to school. Since our room and board were provided, we knew our small store of additional funds would fairly well see us through our summer stay. But shortly after our arrival, Koinonia—which is supported solely by contributions from interested groups and individuals—hit one of its periodic financial crises. Along with other members of the Koinonia family we were called into emergency prayer to seek God's grace in meeting Koinonia's immediate needs.

Alice and I prayed earnestly with the others but that eighty-five dollars kept getting in the way. We quickly agreed we had no right to hold back money which we did not need until September, when Koinonia needed it in July. So we gave the eighty-five dollars plus a small additional sum to help meet the crisis, in the quiet confidence that when we needed it, it would come back to us. Now, a few weeks later, such a time had arrived. Hugging our poverty to ourselves, like a secret, we waited expectantly for God to provide the necessary cash for our trip to Star Island.

Although not conscious of it at the time, we were utilizing one of the most powerful levers of faith available to the Christian. In our small way we had given "all that we had" to help meet Koinonia's financial emergency. If I can say such a thing and not seem irreverent, we had "backed God into a corner." We had done all we could when called upon, and now, with the confidence born of that momentary total commitment, we simply

56

knew God would respond to our present need. Not always have we been so trusting.

But commitment of this kind has a tremendous boosting effect upon one's faith and assurance in God's providential care. Ours may have been an audacious, impractical act when judged by human standards, but it was one which lifted us to a high level of spiritual expectancy. *Such an act of faith paves the way for miracles.* The New Testament makes this clear in the story of the healing of the Roman centurion's servant.[2] From experience the centurion knew the power of his own word over his soldiers. "I say to one, 'Go', and he goes, and another 'Come', and he comes, and to my slave, 'Do this', and he does it." He recognized Jesus had this same kind of authority and submitted to it by telling Him that He need not come personally to pray for his servant. "Only say the word, and I know my servant will be healed." His extravagant faith brought not only healing to his servant, but also praise from the lips of Jesus.

The healing of a woman who had suffered from a hemorrhage for twelve years illustrates the same truth.[3] Reaching out to Jesus, she said, "If I only touch his garment, I shall be made well." This act of faith, this straining through the crowd to touch His seamless robe, set up the miracle. A foolish, irrational act, at least by normal standards of behavior, but it allowed her great need to come in contact with Jesus' great power. She was healed.

"Who was it that touched me?" Jesus asked. "Someone touched me, for I perceive that power has gone forth from me." This is the only case recorded in the Gospels where the miracle was accomplished without Jesus' deliberate participation. It is a spiritual law that when sufficient faith is present, our needs are met out of God's great abundance. "According to your faith be it unto you."[4]

2. Matthew 8:8-10
3. Matthew 9:20-23; Luke 8:45-46
4. Matthew 9:29

So we came to the final week-end before the trip to Star Island with full faith but an empty purse. Although we planned to attend church in Baltimore before leaving for Star Island, I had no money to retrieve my Sunday suit from the local dry cleaners. We checked Friday's and Saturday's mail with unusual care. Many times before money had arrived unexpectedly through the mail just in time to meet some urgent need. But not this time.

Still trusting that the Lord would provide, I took from Koinonia's bookshelf Rufus Moseley's book, *Perfect Everything*, to re-acquaint myself with his experience of the Holy Spirit. When the time came for us to receive, I wanted to be ready. Alone in my room Saturday afternoon, I began to read. At the beginning of his chapter dealing with the baptism in the Holy Spirit, I stumbled across a key sentence: "The baptism of the Holy Spirit is a gift to be received and not an attainment to be rewarded." [5]

Suddenly, my faith soared sky-high! I became aware that we had fallen into the very subtle trap of trying to be *worthy* to receive, as if by self-effort we could induce God's special attention and blessing. I immediately felt such an overpowering sense of the presence of God that had I known then what I know now I would have received the gift of the Holy Spirit, with speaking in tongues, then and there. Even so, I was very close and I knew it was a harbinger of greater things to come.

That evening, just before the dinner hour, Miss Gladys Falshaw arrived. A former Anglican missionary to India, this delightful, Spirit-filled Englishwoman was in demand the country over as a retreat leader. A guest at Koinonia during the summer, she was returning from leading a nearby church retreat. I took her luggage at the front door and we started up to her room while she chatted gaily in her clipped, British accent, telling me how wonderful the retreat had been. Then she stopped me on the stairs.

5. Rufus Moseley in *Perfect Everything*, p. 59, MacAlester Park Publishing Co., St. Paul, Minnesota, used by permission.

"I say, Don, do you and Alice need any money? The people at the retreat were so generous in their offering that I feel I received much more than I should have. I must share my good fortune."

To my surprise I found myself saying, "Why don't you give a contribution to Koinonia, Gladys? The Foundation always needs money." And we continued on to her room where I deposited her luggage.

Back in my own room preparing for dinner I knew it was false pride which kept me from admitting our need. I simply had not had the courage to admit we were flat broke. I could have kicked myself.

As Alice and I came downstairs to dinner a few minutes later I glanced at my watch. It was 6:15 p.m. and the cleaners closed at 7:00 p.m. I turned to Alice. "If something doesn't happen pretty soon, the Lord will have to be content with my worshipping in shirtsleeves tomorrow."

After dinner I was arranging chairs in the library in preparation for the evening worship service, when Gladys appeared at the door and beckoned to me. She took my hand and pressed something into it. "I don't care what you say, the Lord tells me to give you this. You simply must accept it with no argument." Then she quickly turned away. I looked down at my hand to see two twenty-dollar bills smiling up at me.

God had acknowledged the final fleece, and bread cast upon the waters weeks before had returned. I made it to the cleaners five minutes before closing time and the next day worshipped the Lord literally clothed in an answered prayer. And I knew we had an appointment with the Holy Spirit awaiting us at Star Island.

CHAPTER EIGHT

Keeping a Divine Appointment

NINE MILES OFF THE COAST OF Portsmouth, New Hampshire, the Isles of Shoals thrust their bald, rocky heads barely above the waters of the Atlantic. With the afternoon sun warm on our backs, we stood on the deck of the small ferry which regularly plied the waters between them and the mainland and watched the small cluster of islands draw near. Star Island, the largest, was easily recognized by the large rambling old hotel which stood half way up its rocky slope. Behind and to one side of the hotel, on the highest point of the island, was a tiny stone chapel, complete with colonial bell tower. Isolated from the rest of the world, Star Island was the ideal place for a week-long religious retreat. As we stepped off the boat and started up the winding walk to the hotel, I had a momentary feeling that we were treading on holy ground. The inspiration of the next few days abundantly confirmed that feeling.

One morning a group of us stood chatting with Rufus Moseley following an address he had given on the Holy Spirit. Someone asked, "Brother Rufus, what do you consider the greatest barrier preventing people from receiving the baptism in the Holy Spirit?" Without a moment's hesitation he replied, "Fear of public opinion."

Rufus' reply was as accurate as it was brief. More than we are willing to admit, we are creatures of conformity, especially in regard to our religion. Too many of us have inherited strong denominational prejudices which blind us to the truth found in other Christian traditions. Until recently the doctrine of the baptism in the

Holy Spirit and speaking in tongues was associated with denominations which are "different"; which build their churches on the wrong side of the tracks. To seek the pentecostal experience is, therefore, to become fair game for the advocates of the status quo.

Many refuse to seek for this very reason; fear of public opinion. But the promise is to those who "ask" and "seek" and "knock", not to those who desire to avoid criticism. In spite of the great outpouring of the Holy Spirit across protestantism these days, the baptism in the Holy Spirit is still enough of a departure from the religious norm that anyone experiencing it will have his critics. This is a part of the cost of spiritual power.

The next to the last night of the camp had been set aside as an all-night-of-prayer. After supper that evening Harald Bredesen approached us.

"Some folks want to get together tonight to pray for the Holy Spirit. You and Alice want to come?"

We certainly did! About 9:00 p.m. we gathered in one of the small stone cabins near the hotel for prayer. In addition to the half dozen who were "seeking", there were the Spirit-filled friends who were to pray for us. They included Harald Bredesen, Dr. and Mrs. Alden Newman of Bridgeport, Connecticut, and Wyllis and Sybil Mae Archer, faith missionaries to Mexico, home on furlough.

We began an informal time of sharing and worship. There were quiet prayers of thanksgiving and praise. We sang some familiar hymns together and the spirit of our worship deepened. There came a profound sense of the peace and presence of God. Someone began praying in tongues, and I listened intently to the beautiful, expressive flow of language. Although I could not understand a word, it was unmistakably reverent and adoring, and something within my own spirit responded to that adoration.

Under the conviction of the Holy Spirit one woman who was seeking the baptism began to weep. In broken sentences interspersed with sobbing she related certain

61

acts of selfishness and deceit. One of the Spirit-filled friends sitting by her sought to comfort her with assurances of God's love and understanding. Regaining her composure the woman asked the group to pray that God would forgive her. Prayer was offered and in humility she accepted God's forgiveness. With a sudden burst of joyous sound she began to praise God in song. She had a magnificent voice and the melody simply rocked the little cabin. There were no words, just a beautiful rising melody, full of joy.

A few minutes later those ministering to us laid hands on our heads and began to pray—some in English, others in tongues. Someone quietly quoted Jesus' words, "Receive ye the Holy Spirit." [1] The hands on my head began to vibrate gently, as if they were charged with an electric current. Deeply moved by the prayer going on around me, I found myself repeating quietly, "Thank you, Lord. Thank you."

Harald Bredesen leaned close and explained how the Holy Spirit would prompt me to speak words and syllables of praise which I would not be able to understand, and when this happened I was to speak them out. I felt a strange sensation on my lips and tongue but no words came. Then foreign-sounding words and syllables began popping up in my mind. At first I dismissed this, assuming I was either making them up or engaging in a bit of mental mimicry of the tongues being spoken around me. But after a minute or two I opened my mouth and experimentally spoke a few syllables. I felt rather foolish, but then more words came tumbling out. I listened with a kind of detachment as I continued to speak. I could start or stop at will but had no control of the language. The words I spoke had a flow and accent all their own. About the same time I became aware that Alice, kneeling next to me, was also speaking in tongues, in a language quite different from mine.

What an altogether strange experience it was! Al-

1. John 20:22

most as if I were two persons; both observer and participant. There was joy and release within my spirit, but intellectually it made no sense. Then I recalled the words of Paul, "If I pray in a tongue, my *spirit* prays but my *mind* is unfruitful . . . for one who prays in a tongue speaks not to men but to God; for no one understands him, but he utters mysteries in the Spirit." [2] In my college classes these Scriptures were cited as arguments against the use of tongues, being interpreted in a negative sense only. Now I suddenly understood what Paul was really describing. He was describing a kind of prayer originating, not with the mind, but from the depths of the spirit, at a level not to be comprehended by the intellect. It was prayer "beyond" reason.

The spiritual principle illustrated here has application beyond speaking in tongues. One does not have to "understand" all that God desires to do in and through him. More spiritual progress is made by faith and trust than by reason and analysis. *It is faith, not reason, which initiates spiritual experience.* In the New Testament the experience of God's power comes first. It was not a carefully worked out theology which made the apostles' ministry dynamic; it was first-hand experience of the Holy Spirit. As Paul said, "My speech and my message were not in plausible words of wisdom, *but in demonstration of the Spirit and power,* that your faith might not rest in the wisdom of men but in the power of God." [3]

So it is with us. Believing God's promise we ask for and receive baptism in the Holy Spirit. Intellectual confirmation of the experience may not come until later. Indeed, the ordinary mind, more skeptical than trusting and more accustomed to the tempter's voice than to the whispers of God, is scarcely a trustworthy instrument for passing judgment on spiritual experience. "The unspiritual man does not receive the gifts of the Spirit of God for they are folly to him, and he is not able to under-

2. I Corinthians 14:14, 14:2
3. I Corinthians 2:4-5

63

stand them for they are *spiritually* (not intellectually) discerned." [4]

Praying in tongues, I quickly came to understand, is not for the purpose of educating the intellect, but for *liberating the spirit in worship.*

After those seeking had received the baptism in the Holy Spirit, we found ourselves standing in a circle with hands joined, singing glorious hymns of praise to God. Then one voice lifted above the others, singing in tongues. The rest of us fell silent as the haunting words and melody filled the little cabin. The song died away and the interpretation came through Harald Bredesen. It was poetic prophecy, majestic and loving in tone, and spoke of God's great love for His children; of His longing to pour out His Spirit upon all. It was a burdened prophecy, pleading for the redemption of a world heading for destruction because it was blind to His love. We listened in tears.

Then it was all over. The meeting ended as quietly as it had begun. I glanced at my watch and was surprised to find we had been together for over three hours. One by one we slipped away from that hallowed little cabin. Later that night, after Alice was asleep, I sat by the window in our room and watched the moon trace her silver signature across the face of the sea. How was I to fit this strange and wonderful experience into my Christian life? How was it to be explained to others? I sensed somehow that the most important task of my life would be that of trying to communicate the truth of this experience to others. But how? I fell asleep, still praising God with rivers of foreign-sounding phrases pouring through my thoughts.

No profound religious experience can be maintained at peak intensity for long. Dawn brought not only the cold light of day but the cold light of reason as well. I began to probe, sift and analyze what had happened —and thus to doubt. So I had spoken some strange-

4. I Corinthians 2:14

sounding words and phrases, so what? How could I be sure it wasn't just some kind of meaningless babble? How could I be sure it was actually "speaking in tongues" as the Scriptures recorded? The warm assurance I had the night before suddenly evaporated.

I readily admitted the reality of the Presence of God in our worship. No doubt about the genuine contrition and subsequent joy of the woman who sang in the Spirit. In fact, I could accept everything which happened to the others but doubted my own experience. I sought out Harald Bredesen and confronted him with my problem. He understood and quickly related how nearly everyone experienced similar doubts following the experience. He even confessed to having experienced the same doubts himself.

"But this is a time for standing fast on the Word of God, Don," he insisted. "The Scriptures clearly promise the gift of the Holy Spirit, don't they?" I nodded. "And the Scriptural evidence of receiving the Holy Spirit is speaking in tongues, isn't it?" I nodded again.

"Well, this is precisely what happened to you last night," Harald said. "But if you still feel dubious about your experience, then take it on my word. I *know* you spoke in tongues. I haven't the slightest doubt about your experience. So for now, trust *my* faith if you cannot trust your own. The time will soon come when you will look back on last night and know that it was there, in that little cabin, that God granted your desire and filled you with His Holy Spirit."

Subsequent experience proved Harald was absolutely correct. In fact, I quickly discovered that in addition to the universal doubts we all have—which come from the stubborn intellect which doubts everything supernatural—I was also fighting my own preconceived ideas. Through our long months of seeking I had unconsciously developed a mental picture of what I *thought* should happen how I *thought* I should feel. I had come to expect some highly dramatic, ecstatic experience; some

65

kind of vision or great flash of light. By contrast, though profoundly moving, mine was a relatively quiet experience.

So in spite of initial doubts it soon became clear that truly this *was* God moving in my life more powerfully than ever before and that I had made entry into a new and deeper spiritual dimension, clearly marked by the experience of praying in a language utterly unknown to me.

We had kept our appointment with the Holy Spirit.

CHAPTER NINE

Down from the Mountaintop

THE CAMP ENDED the next night and the following morning we caught the ferry back to the mainland to make the long drive back to Baltimore. Rufus Moseley was a passenger in our car and enlivened the journey with his gentle good humor and constant praise to God.[1] As we swept along the parkway near Boston, he began praising God for the good road. Then he began offering thanksgiving that we were not only on a good paved highway, but that we were all on "the King's highway, heading for heaven". We began singing hymns and praising God in the spirit, and glory seemed to fill the car.

I can still hear Rufus' clear, high voice crying, "Thank you Jesus! Hallelujah! We do love you, Lord!" His uninhibited joy in the Holy Spirit was sometimes a source of embarrassment to long-faced Christians. Once, after hearing him speak, a resentful, dour-faced woman complained, "But Brother Rufus, do you think Jesus ever smiled?"

"Sister, I don't know about that," Rufus beamed, "but he sure fixed me so I can!"

Rufus was something of a food faddist—almost vegetarian in his eating habits. He felt, with some justification, that most Americans are eating themselves to death. Once a portly lady, concerned about certain Old

1. Few men in modern times have approached the degree of spiritual union with Jesus Christ experienced by this choice servant of God. His personal testimony is recorded in two books: *Manifest Victory*, Harpers, N.Y., now out of print, and *Perfect Everything*, MacAlester Park Publishing Co., St. Paul, Minnesota.

Testament food restrictions, asked him, "Brother Rufus, can we eat pork and still get to Heaven?"

"Sure," Rufus replied, "and the more you eat the quicker you'll get there!"

At noon we stopped at a roadside restaurant, and I watched with interest as Rufus ordered a large bowl of fruit salad. When it arrived, he reached into a bag he carried with him and brought out some raw peanuts and a nut grinder. Carefully he ground the peanuts into a small heap atop the bowl of fruit. Next, out came a small jar of honey which Rufus poured generously over the concoction in front of him. He knew I was watching and waited for my comment.

I looked at my plate of hot roast beef and then at the gooey mess before him and smiled. "Brother Rufus, I'll bet I enjoy my meal more than you enjoy yours."

"You may enjoy your meals at mealtime," Rufus retorted, "but I enjoy mine all the time between."

When some critic ridiculed Rufus' fondness for raw peanuts, one who knew him well replied, "If I could get what Moseley has by eating raw peanuts, I'd eat them by the ton."

Back at Koinonia we packed for the return to Phillips University. Wyllis and Sybil Mae Archer, now on their way back to Mexico, were to travel with us. We planned to stop overnight at a Camp Farthest Out in North Carolina, where the Archers had been invited to tell of their mission work.

Leaving Baltimore we headed down the beautiful Skyline Drive which winds its way across the mountains of Virginia. An early fall was in evidence with some of the trees already lightly brushed with flaming color. The Archers sat in the back, holding hands and savoring every mile of the trip. In their service on the mission field they often endured long periods of separation and thus reveled in this opportunity for simple companionship.

Early in their marriage Sybil Mae had been stricken with an illness which left her an invalid. Then the Lord marvelously healed her and baptized her in the Holy Spirit, providing her with a testimony so powerful that Wyllis—at that time the plodding pastor of a small church—resigned his pastorate in embarrassment. After he too was filled with the Holy Spirit, they were led to establish a faith work in Mexico. Some of their experiences there could have come straight from the Book of Acts.

Once Sybil Mae was teaching a group of Mexican children a Bible lesson as they sat together beside a stream. The lesson was from Luke, chapter 5, where Jesus told the disciples to cast their nets on the other side of the boat and they caught so many fish the boat began to sink. Suddenly a couple of mischievous boys exploded in unbelieving laughter, ridiculing the story. Then the other students began to laugh and join in the derision. Tears came to Sybil Mac's eyes as she halted the lesson and bowed her head in agonizing prayer.

"All at once," she recalled, "the Holy Spirit moved mightily upon me and spoke strong words of rebuke to the unbelieving children. When they laughed all the harder, I suddenly found myself picking up a pail resting by the stream's edge and boldly thrusting it into the water. In a strange and unexpected frenzy, a large school of minnows churned the water nearby and, as if on signal, swam with a rush *into the pail.* I pulled the pail from the stream and poured hundreds of slippery, wriggling minnows at the feet of the astonished children saying, '*Now* will you believe God's word?' The children began to weep and slipped to their knees pleading for forgiveness."

A few days later the Archers conducted a baptismal service at the spot, immersing a number of young converts, including some from Sybil Mae's class. The new young Christians came up out of the baptismal waters filled with the Holy Spirit, praising God in unknown tongues and prophesying. This experience more nearly typifies the pattern suggested in Peter's sermon at Pentecost than any I've heard. "Repent and be baptized," he instructed, "and you will receive the gift of the Holy Spirit" (Acts 2:38).

Arriving at the North Carolina CFO we ate dinner, attended the evening services and retired. We were assigned adjoining rooms in the same cabin. About midnight I was awakened by Wyllis and Sybil Mae talking in the next room. I slipped out of bed and joined them to discover Wyllis in great physical discomfort, suffering from what he thought to be indigestion. He sat on a chair with a blanket draped over his shoulders.

We chatted a few minutes and prayed together. With a shaky laugh Wyllis stood up. "I don't think God wants me to endure much more of this pain." He closed his eyes and tugged the blanket closer around his shoulders. Suddenly he gasped and his eyes opened wide. His face broke into a beautiful smile as he gazed toward the ceiling. I had the distinct feeling he was seeing a world which we could not see. Then he collapsed across the bed, fatally stricken by a heart attack.

Wyllis' sudden death stunned us all, but Sybil Mae proved a tower of strength. Next morning she stood before the assembled campers and gave the most inspiring testimony to the love and grace of Jesus Christ I ever heard. With tears streaming down her cheeks she told how God had blessed their lives and honored their ministry. She thanked Him for their wonderful life together and for the knowledge that Wyllis was now safe at home with the Lord. As she finished, a reverent hush fell over the meeting and no one moved or spoke for long minutes afterward.

After a brief memorial service, arrangements were made to ship Wyllis' body to Texas where the Archer children resided. Then we continued our journey, this time with Sybil Mae riding in the back seat alone. That two-day trip was a constant miracle of inspiration. Sybil Mae was literally upheld on a sea of prayer and praise. She admitted that God had been preparing her for what happened. Just a few weeks before, while meeting with friends for prayer, prophecy was spoken over her concerning *her* future ministry, with no mention of Wyllis. "Always before," she sighed, "prophecy had come for both of us." So she had had a premonition of her husband's death. "But how like our wonderful Jesus," she concluded, "to give us those last precious days together. It was like a second honeymoon."

*   *   *   *

No two people's experience in the Holy Spirit is exactly the same, for God leads us in individual paths for our own good. Usually, Christians who are newly-filled with the Holy Spirit have the encouragement and fellowship provided by a prayer group of other Spirit-filled Christians where their initial experience can be confirmed and deepened. But like it or not, we were immediately thrust back into the scholastic life of the college campus where no prayer fellowship was available to us. We felt cut off from spiritual reality, but nevertheless were determined to hold on.

Between classes I would slip into the tiny prayer chapel on campus. Alone in the room I would speak aloud words and phrases I recalled from that precious night, wondering what they meant—wondering if they were actually words in a language which could be understood by someone, somewhere. I even searched my Greek textbook and Greek New Testament, looking for words which sounded similar to the "unknown tongue".

Time and again, however, I was tempted to reject the entire experience and retreat back into conventional religious orthodoxy. Then one morning, in a mood more despondent than usual, I made my way into the little chapel to pour out my complaint to the Lord. As I had done many times before, I began repeating over and over the one phrase in tongues which seemed the most real, but wondering all the while if it were Spirit-given or just "me". All at once the Holy Spirit moved with a gentle insistence upon my lips and tongue, and I found myself praising God with long, poetic-sounding passages of speech in a language I had never known or heard.

71

Somewhere deep inside I felt a kind of "letting go", as if some part of me which had still been held in reserve, was finally being given to God. My prayer in tongues seemed entirely fitting to express my gratitude to God. Almost lost in an overwhelming spirit of worship and praise, I recognized my voice changing from language to language. At times the speech sounded oriental, other times slavic. At one time I had the impression I was speaking a very ancient tongue, as if there were prayers being prayed through me which were centuries old.

The great freedom in praying in tongues which I found in that little prayer chapel has never left me. Sometimes it seems to flow day and night, just under the surface of consciousness. It is as if I were in touch with the Holy Spirit whether consciously aware of it or not. Although at times I rebel and turn away from the Holy Spirit's leading, the moment I turn back to God in contrition and worship, praise to Him in tongues comes welling up. I find a precious intimacy in this kind of prayer which seems missing in all other forms.

From that time on I never doubted the validity of my experience with tongues, but there still lay ahead my years of seminary training. They were years of both joy and frustration. Joy over the times I knew the Holy Spirit was working in my life and in the lives of others on the campus; and frustration over the tedious months of difficult study, much of which was so in contrast to the warm devotional approach to the Christian faith I believed to be so essential.

Although I applied myself diligently to the curriculum, I never became reconciled to what I felt was the seminary's determined effort to major in minor matters. Critical and rationalistic explorations in the fields of theology and Biblical criticism may fascinate many students, but such an approach to faith understandably creates a great gulf between the young minister and the average church member in his congregation. Discussions ad infinitum on the documentary theory of the Pentateuch, or on whether or not the book of Isaiah was authored by the prophet or is a combination work of Isaiah, Deutero-Isaiah and Trito-Isaiah; or on the question of Pauline authorship of certain New Testament epistles, all may excite the imagination of the specialist in Biblical criticism, but they are mighty thin gruel for the troubled Christian who would seek solace in God's word.

It came as no surprise, therefore, upon my graduation and acceptance of a full-time pastorate, to discover both from my own experience and from my association with other ministers, that while most churches want the prestige of a seminary-trained man, they tend to tolerate, rather than appreciate, most of his seminary "wisdom".

CHAPTER TEN

Fire on the Campus

IN THE FALL of 1953 a college classmate and I began to pray daily for the Holy Spirit to fall on Phillips University. We had shared our Star Island experience with him and his wife and now both were seeking the baptism in the Holy Spirit. One night we attended a revival service being held in a pentecostal church not far from the campus. At the close of the service we all went forward for prayer. Although the pentecostal folk were loving and sympathetic, the noisy confusion and loud praying effected my friends the same as it once had me. They were unable to respond to the Holy Spirit in such surroundings. Later the wife told me that as she knelt at the altar one well-meaning sister whispered in her ear, "Dearie, if you'll take off your lipstick and make-up the Lord will give you His Spirit". We agreed this was not an essential prerequisite for the Holy Spirit baptism.

As it turned out, the Lord ignored our carefully planned efforts and created a situation of His own to begin the outpouring of His power. One night in the early spring three of us got together to study New Testament Greek. One student happened to be a young pentecostal minister enrolled at Phillips, and it was in his apartment that we met. Soon tiring of the difficult assignment, we turned to discussing matters more directly pertaining to the faith we shared. When the third student discovered that the other two of us had received the baptism in the Holy Spirit, he confessed to a great longing for the experience and asked us to pray for him.

Laying our books aside we stood beside Roy's chair.

With some hesitancy I placed my hands on his head as we asked the Lord to grant his desire. I felt a strange vibration in my hands as they rested on his head. Roy began to shake and tremble in the chair and to pray aloud for God to bless him. I suggested he stop praying in English and let the Holy Spirit give him a new language of praise. Almost before the words were out of my mouth he burst forth speaking in tongues, tears of joy streaming down his cheeks. He jumped to his feet praising God at the top of his voice.

The immediacy of his response was almost more "pentecostal" than I had bargained for, and for a moment I had to stifle a panicky urge to bolt for the door. "Now look what you've done," I silently berated myself. I could just see the neighbors in the adjoining apartments telephoning the police or coming around to investigate. What an embarrassing incident that would be for all of us! After all, my own response to receiving the Holy Spirit had been as tame as weak tea compared to Roy's.

No one came, however, and the look on Roy's face as he paced back and forth across the room singing and praising God soon quieted my uneasiness.

Some minutes later he sat down on the couch opposite me, his entire body still vibrating under the Spirit's power so that the whole couch began to shake. He looked puzzled. "You know, one part of me does not want to accept what has happened. I could doubt the reality of this experience right now if I would let myself." I nodded and described the similar feeling following my own experience.

Roy's baptism marked the beginning of an outpouring of the Holy Spirit on a number of university students. The couple with whom I had attended the pentecostal revival service were next. One day the three of us parked in my car at the bank of a river near town. After concentrated prayer for the girl seemed fruitless, I momentarily gave up in despair. "I don't know what else to say or how else to help you." So there we sat, staring out across the river.

As the girl apologized for her lack of progress, her husband took a Bible from the glove compartment and let it fall open on his lap. He sat upright when the words seemed to leap from the page. "Behold, if the vision tarry, wait for it. It will surely come" (Habakkuk 2:3). We laughed and thanked God together for the startling relevance of the passage, then suddenly the girl blurted out several words in an unknown tongue. Soon torrents of praise were cascading from her lips.

The next day her husband experienced the baptism in a quiet, almost emotionless manner. He spoke clearly and distinctly a number of foreign-sounding phrases, but for some reason—perhaps because his wife's experience had been more dramatic—he was immediately subjected to great doubt. "I don't think I was speaking in tongues; it was just sounds I made up! Besides, I don't feel any different! This whole business has made me feel like a fool!" Then he began to ridicule the few words and phrases he had spoken. I was concerned, but as we continued praying, prophecy confirmed that his experience, like his wife's, was from the Lord. "Behold, my manservant upon whom has been bestowed the promised gift. The Lord sent forth disciples, not one by one but two by two, and so shall ye go forth, man and wife together, to minister in My holy name."

That experience taught me not to become disturbed at anyone's first reaction to the manifestation of God's power, however unexpected. Just days later we witnessed a dramatic change in this young man's attitude. Deeply immersed in the Spirit, he prayed fluently and beautifully in tongues. No trace of doubt remained. I recognized his prayer language as Spanish, although too many years had passed since my study of the language to understand much of it. I did clearly hear the phrase, "sangre de Cristo" or "blood of Christ" repeated twice. He later admitted he had no knowledge of Spanish and was unaware that he was praying in any known tongue.

Two additional students joined our group as a result of a dramatic spiritual healing. Under a doctor's care, one was suffering from a serious eye affliction and was scheduled for surgery as soon as the semester ended. One night, unknown to him, we offered earnest believing prayer to God for his healing. A few days later Eddie cornered me in the campus coffee shop to tell me his eye difficulty had remarkably disappeared. Just the day before he had returned to the doctor's office and examination revealed no trace of the affliction. He suspected we had prayed for him.

That very night he came to our meeting and received the promised gift of the Holy Spirit. Returning to his dormitory room, he decided to wait up for his roommate to tell what had happened, but instead fell asleep. Later, his roommate came in and being anxious to hear first hand about the meeting where "people pray in tonuges", nudged Eddie to wake him. Still in his sleep, Eddie began praising God aloud in tongues. After a minute he awoke with a big smile.

"Say, do I have something to tell you!"

"You don't have to tell me," came the startled reply, "I already know!" The next night Eddie's roommate also received the baptism in the Holy Spirit.

But reaction to the moving of the Holy Spirit on the campus was not long in coming. Despite our admonitions, one girl in our group felt she must testify to a professor whom she greatly admired. Not only was the professor ice-cold in his rejection of her testimony—"Are you claiming that because you think you speak in tongues, you're more spiritual than I am?"—but he also sternly lectured her for getting involved with a "bunch of fanatics". Deeply hurt by his rejection the girl refused to participate further in the prayer meetings. The professor who rebuked her then reported the incident to the president of the University.

How grateful we were for the gracious attitude of President Briggs and his wife! Both were sympathetic to the operation of spiritual gifts, and Mrs. Briggs even encouraged students who questioned her about the group to visit our meetings. One girl came and sat quietly through an evening with us. During the meeting tears came to her eyes as she testified to an overwhelming awareness of the love of God. But when I saw her the next day on campus her defenses were up. "I appreciate being invited to your meeting," she said, "and I'm convinced that what happens there is wholly of God. But you're playing with dynamite and I don't want to get involved."

Like others, she was frightened by the wave of rumors which began to circulate around the campus. We were accused of holding seances and practicing voodoo. Some claimed we were experimenting with hypnotism and were putting one another into trances. It was even said that we turned out all the lights and held wild sex parties. Some wanted to circulate a petition to have us expelled from the University.

Although shocked and saddened by this turn of events, we did not blame our student friends. It is natural to criticize what one doesn't understand, and Satan has a way of using the ignorance of friends to discredit what God is doing. Happily, the rumors died out almost as quickly as they began and the campus furor lasted only a few weeks.

During the controversy the Briggs' sympathetic understanding was most encouraging. "Dr. Briggs and I are simply delighted with what has been happening," Mrs Briggs told me. "For years we have prayed for the Spirit of God to stir this campus. We hope you will not be too upset or offended by the reaction of those who do not understand."

As the originator of the group on campus I was questioned closely by a special committee appointed from the faculty. These men were deeply sincere and committed Christians. They were gracious in their questioning and did not criticize me personally. Their concern was related to the impression such novel spiritual experiences might have on the students as a whole, and more specifically the prospect that what was happening on campus might adversely affect the financial support furnished the college by constituent churches. They also felt it was necessary to consider whether, in light of my "pentecostal experience", I should be allowed to continue preaching in my student church.

"In fact, Don," one faculty member said kindly, "we find it hard to understand why you wish to remain in the Christian church since your theology and experience are so foreign to our historic position."

"I can understand your concern," I replied, "yet each morning at nine o'clock I hear a lecture reflecting one religious viewpoint or position. At ten o'clock another professor's lecture reflects a different theology. Then, in the afternoon my professor may strongly disagree with the other two. Yet you men serve on the same faculty and seem happy in the same denomination.

"I'll admit," I continued, "that what is happening in our prayer meetings may seem strange to some; yet we claim to be a 'New Testament people' and the baptism in the Holy Spirit with speaking in tongues is clearly revealed in the New Testament. I cannot help but appeal to the New Testament as my authority."

I think I had Divine help in my answers, for in the end the committee took no action. I was sent a letter stating that while the committee did not endorse what was happening, there had always been room for wide divergence of personal theology within our denomination. And since the experiences were largely of a personal nature, it was not the committee's place to pass judgment on them. Neither would any steps be taken to interfere with my serving a student church.

While the matter was still under deliberation by the faculty committee, we drove to Oklahoma City to seek the counsel and prayers of friends. There we learned that Rufus Moseley, whose life and testimony had meant so much to us, was in the hospital near death. We went to see him. He seemed more in the Spirit than in the body when we arrived, as though his frail body (he was over

79

80) could scarcely contain the radiance of his triumphant spirit. Every few words his conversation would be interrupted with thanksgiving to the Jesus he adored, sometimes in English, sometimes in tongues. He had heard of the campus outpouring and said he had been thanking Jesus for our ministry.

When I confessed our dismay over the wild rumors and possibility of critical action by the faculty committee, he said kindly, "Don, if you decide the cost of witnessing to the power of the Holy Spirit is too great; if you decide the baptism in the Holy Spirit is not meant for now and silence your witness, your ministry will be robbed of much of its power."

His parting benediction I shall never forget. "Goodbye," he said, "and in my prayers I shall constantly see you receiving Jesus' best and highest." We were reluctant to leave, for we knew we would never see him again. A few weeks later he slipped into heaven.

Rufus' words have proved prophetic, for my ministry has been effective only when I remain faithful in my testimony to the power of the Holy Spirit. The times when I have silenced my witness and compromised my convictions have been times spent in the valley of dry bones, barren and ineffective.

During the days when criticism of our prayer group was running high, discussions were enlivened by the beginning of the TV broadcasts showing the healing services of evangelist, Oral Roberts. Interestingly enough, Roberts' healing ministry began while he was a student at Phillips University and serving as pastor of a local Pentecostal Holiness church. He conducted his first large healing service in a downtown auditorium where University graduation exercises were also held. Roberts himself had been miraculously healed of tuberculosis in both lungs while still in his teens.

The reaction of most young ministerial intellectuals to such a ministry was highly critical, even indignant. Roberts was called everything from a publicity-seeking fanatic to an outright fraud. After all, most ministerial students spend years in college and seminary learning all the reasons why miracles can't happen any more.

But the power of the Holy Spirit cannot be so easily dismissed. One day I stood outside a classroom patiently trying to refute a fellow classmate's persistent denunciation of Oral Roberts' ministry. He claimed Roberts had paid cohorts who followed the campaigns from one city to another, walking through the healing line and claiming miraculous cures to deceive the public. Another student joined us during the critical tirade. He listened until it was finished.

"I know *one* woman who wasn't paid to testify," he said. "My aunt. She contracted gangrene from a foot infection and was scheduled for surgery to have all her toes removed. The day before she was to enter the hospital she attended an Oral Roberts meeting. She was instantly healed and still has all her toes."

My glib classmate had no answer.

CHAPTER ELEVEN

Learning the Hard Way

GIVEN THE PROPER SET OF CIRCUMSTANCES any minister can have what is popularly called a "successful" ministry. All he needs is a church location on the growing edge of a city, surrounded by middle-income homes filled with middle-income families who are eager to put down roots in their middle-income suburb by joining all the organizations representative of their middle-income community life. In such a situation, statistical success for a church is practically guaranteed. With a modest amount of loyal endeavor there soon comes into being a growing congregation, lovely new church buildings and an ever-swelling budget, all wrapped up in a happy program of social and religious activities. Such churches dot the suburban landscape from coast to coast, each one giving heed to the proven philosophy that to be successful the church must follow its flock to the suburbs where the sheep who have strayed from the downtown churches can be brought back into the fold.

Yet in the midst of such easy success there are danger signals flying everywhere. What passes for evangelism may be nothing more than combing the neighborhood for ready-made church members. Preoccupation with building programs and fat financial reports, plus days and nights of thriving activity, lull us into believing that the will of God is being fulfilled in people's lives simply because "everything is going so well". I know, because I was the minister in such a church for almost five years.

Fresh out of seminary I was called to Washington, D.C., to serve the remnant of a congregation which had disposed of its downtown property and moved to the Maryland suburbs. In five years we saw the congregation grow from a handful to almost two hundred. The annual budget increased from $7,000 to almost $25,000. A beautiful $25,000 parsonage was erected and a $100,000 church unit as well. Our church was the picture of success. Outwardly we had everything going for us. In on the ground floor of a developing suburban community, we rubbed our hands in glee with the establishment of every new subdivision. The town was moving our way.

Our people's enthusiasm over the church's statistical prospects was quite understandable. However, I was concerned with my failure to introduce a deeper spiritual life which would match the physical growth of the church and its facilities. Several years had passed since I had received the baptism in the Holy Spirit with its transforming effect on my life. I had been able to share the experience with some of my fellow students in seminary and to minister on occasion to interested individuals and groups outside the local church, but introducing such a ministry into a successful suburbanite congregation proved a different matter. In the midst of easy statistical success, spiritual truths become decidedly intangible.

The fault lay not so much with my church people as with me. Generous-hearted, loving and eager to be "good church members", they were puzzled by my dissatisfaction with the way things were going. Spiritual self-discipline, power in prayer and an ever-increasing commitment to Jesus Christ were the things I desperately wanted to impart, but inevitably these were crowded to one side. There was always the pressing competition of the building program, developing property, raising money and working to establish new committees and new programs, to say nothing of the even more difficult task of harmonizing those already in operation. Of more immediate fascination than the power of God were the frequent announcements in the newspaper of proposed new subdivisions and plans for extension of highways and public utilities into our neighborhood. I could not seem to keep

83

our church from conforming to the image of just another "successful" suburban church.

At times I even found my own prideful spirit smirking with satisfaction over our outward growth, but deep inside I knew I was responsible for developing a church disturbingly similar to the Laodicean church in Revelation whom our Lord admonished, *"You say, I am rich, I have prospered and I need nothing, not knowing that you are wretched, pitiable, poor, blind and naked."*[1]

Looking back on those years I am convinced that my "successful" failure at that church stemmed primarily from my lack of honest and forthright witness to the outpouring of the Holy Spirit in my own life.

But while I was unable to render the kind of ministry I had hoped, there were still a few occasions during those years when we experienced the power of God in a most wonderful way.

During our first year in Washington we were constantly beset with minor illnesses. Doctors told us it was due to the radical change in climate. Moving from the dry plains of Oklahoma into the damp and humid Potomac River basin required more than a little adjustment, and for months we endured a succession of colds, flu attacks, sinus infections and even a bout or two with pneumonia.

Then, in February of 1958, a year after our arrival, Alice had a wisdom tooth extracted and the resulting wound refused to heal. In spite of careful medication and return visits to the dentist, infection set in. The dentist referred her to an oral surgeon who lanced the infected area, which by then had spread to the wall of her cheek. Still the difficulty persisted and one afternoon Alice returned from the doctor's office badly shaken.

"He says it has become too serious for him to treat further. He . . . he wants me to go to a cancer specialist." She broke down and wept.

Cancer! That dreadful word struck fear in my heart, and I had to choke back a momentary feeling of panic.

1. Revelation 3:17

After a few minutes we talked quietly, trying to assure one another that the swelling on her jaw was only from the tooth extraction and the appointment with the cancer specialist merely a routine precaution.

Two days later we traveled across town to Georgetown Hospital where we had an appointment with a famed cancer specialist. A sad-eyed, gentle man, he examined Alice thoroughly, checking the X-rays the dentist and oral surgeon had made and then came to the outer office to talk privately with me.

"I don't want to alarm you, Mr. Basham, but you should be informed of what is probably in store for your wife. I want to make a biopsy of the swelling on her jaw to check for malignancy. While I can't say for sure, it is probable that more extensive surgery must follow. I'm afraid we must remove that lump. We will be unable to perform the surgery from within the mouth but must make the incision on the outside, from here to here." Slowly he drew a line along his jaw from just below his ear almost to the point of his chin. I was too stunned to speak, but the worst was yet to come.

"In the event we make such an incision," he continued, "we cannot possibly avoid severing some of the facial nerves which control the muscles around the eye and mouth. This will result in some disfigurement—how much we cannot say for sure—perhaps a drooping eyelid, a corner of the mouth turned down. She will not be able to smile with that side of her face." Seeing the look of dismay on my face, the doctor put his hand on my shoulder. "I'm very sorry, Mr. Basham, but it's best to be prepared ahead of time for these things. Of course we won't know for sure until after the biopsy, but I wanted you to know . . ."

I scarcely heard the last of his words. Major surgery from a tooth extraction? Probable disfigurement? It didn't seem possible!

The kindly doctor thrust a slip of paper into my hand. "I've scheduled an appointment for the biopsy for a week from today. We can do it here in the office. No need to hospitalize your wife until later when . . ." His voice trailed off as Alice came in from the examination room. Thanking the doctor, we hurried out of the hospital. Determined to keep the ugly prognosis to myself, I spoke with forced cheerfulness. "He wants you back a week from today for a biopsy. But if the Lord has His way I don't think the swelling will be there next week."

Time and again in the days which followed we prayed for Alice's healing. In moments of deep faith and prayer, we received strong assurance from the Holy Spirit that everything would turn out all right. But in the long hours between, devils of fear sapped my courage and faith. Those fears were given added power by the appearance on Alice's cheek of a dark, angry blotch, resembling a deeply embedded boil.

The night before the scheduled biopsy we spent long hours in prayer, again receiving assurance from the Holy Spirit that all would be well.

"I'm not sure I want to keep the appointment tomorrow," Alice calmly announced after our prayer time. "I think we're supposed to trust God for my healing."

I was emotionally exhausted over the continual battle with my own fearsome thoughts, and Alice's statement didn't help. I was well aware of the danger of procrastination in such cases. Yet I had to admit that all our guidance seemed to confirm her stand.

"We'll decide tomorrow," I said, still nourishing the faint hope that by tomorrow the miracle of healing would take place.

But the decision I was loathe to make was made for us. We awoke the next morning to find the city caught in the grips of a blinding snowstorm. The doctor's secretary called cancelling the appointment and postponing the biopsy for one week.

Once again our days and nights alternated between fear and faith, trust and torment. Our new parsonage was under construction at the time and I often visited the site. One day I was standing inside the cold shell of the house, staring out the hole where our living room window would be, talking with the building contractor. Somehow the conversation turned to the power of prayer. The builder had not impressed me as a religious man, and I can't recall how the conversation ever developed— but surely the Holy Spirit had a hand in it. To my surprise he began to tell me about his father, who, in addition to helping his son build houses, was pastor of a small church in the northwest part of the city.

He told me how his father, while still a youth, had been severely injured by a kick from a mule. For years following the accident he had been crippled, and the doctors gave him no hope for improvement. Then friends took him to a Pentecostal tent meeting where he was marvelously healed, not only of a broken, twisted back, but of an embarrassing speech impediment as well. As a result of the healing and his subsequent conversion and baptism in the Holy Spirit, he felt called to preach.

Astonished and pleased at the story, I confided to the builder my concern over Alice's condition. I asked if he thought it would be proper for us to visit his father's church and have prayer for her healing. The next day the father, whom everyone called Pastor Marks, accompanied his son to our building site and personally invited me to bring Alice to his church for prayer that very night.

We accepted his invitation and were greatly impressed by the enthusiasm and faith of the small congregation and the earnestness of their prayers on Alice's behalf. Following the special prayer service, during which Pastor Marks anointed Alice's forehead with oil, we made our way home.

Although she felt nothing during the service, later that night Alice was awakened when the power of God, like a strong burning sensation, struck the afflicted area inside her mouth. She knew something wonderful had happened, and the next morning announced happily, "My jaw is not stiff anymore. The inside of my mouth is healed and all the swelling and infection are gone."

It was true and I would have been overjoyed, except

that the ugly, boil-like lump remained on the outside of her cheek. I insisted that we keep the appointment for the biopsy, but once again the appointed day found a howling blizzard visited upon the city. Again the appointment was cancelled and this time Alice refused to make another.

"How much more proof do you want?" she chided me. "My jaw is *healed*, I tell you!"

"But what about that ugly thing on her cheek?" I wondered fearfully. I didn't say anything, but I knew the fears implanted in my mind by the cancer specialist concerning Alice's probable disfigurement—fears which I resolutely refused to share—were blocking my faith and standing in the way of her complete healing. Desperately I asked for concrete guidance from the Holy Spirit to assure me that nothing further would be needed in the way of a doctor's treatment.

"Surely, she will lift up her face without a blemish," came the strong assurance from the Holy Spirit. It was also made plain to us that we were not to return to the cancer specialist.

"Then perhaps some other doctor, Lord?" I asked plaintively, concerned that no avenue of help be neglected. Was I imagining it or was the lump on Alice's cheek growing in size? Two days later we had our answer when Alice returned home following choir practice.

"The choir director noticed this thing on my cheek and gave me the name of a skin specialist. Should I go to him?" We prayed over the doctor's name, and quickly and clearly the answer came. "Go to him, for he is a good man and brings good news."

The next day I found myself in the doctor's outer office waiting, while he examined Alice. I was still fighting the gnawing fear within by determinedly repeating the assurances the Holy Spirit had given. Soon Alice emerged with a small neat bandage covering the place on her cheek. I stood up.

"Well?"

She smiled radiantly and took my hand. "He says it

is nothing unusual at all; just an infection from a stopped-up oil gland. He opened it with a small incision and says in three days I'll never know it was there."

At Alice's words my fear melted like mist before the morning sun. It was all so sudden and yet so undramatic that for days I had to brush away the nagging cobwebs of doubt which would spin themselves across my thoughts in unexpected moments. Today, the only reminder of that ordeal is a tiny, almost invisible scar on Alice's cheek, a scar which creases into an attractive dimple when she smiles her lovely smile.

Often, as I see her face, I remember the words of the cancer specialist as he talked of a six-inch incision and a permanent droop to lip and eye-lid; I remember the days of anguished prayer and the fight for faith; I remember Pastor Marks and his small band of faithful Christians; but most of all I remember the quiet promise of the Holy Spirit, "Surely, she will lift up her face without a blemish." Once again, God was as good as His word.

CHAPTER TWELVE

Blacktop Miracle

THE SPRING OF 1958 saw the completion of our new parsonage and the groundbreaking service for the new church building. Since our move to the suburbs, church services had been held in an old renovated tavern about a mile away. The parsonage was the loveliest home we had ever lived in, and from our front porch we could watch the work progress on the church building some hundred yards away.

The summer passed swiftly and with the arrival of autumn our congregation looked forward with mounting enthusiasm and expectancy to the day when we would move into the new church. Week after week I hammered away in my preaching on the need for spiritual growth and maturity, constantly reminding our people that the new property and building would have little real significance unless we matched them with a new and vital dedication of life and purpose.

"We must open our lives to the power of God and learn to trust Him," I said repeatedly in my sermons. But I wasn't making much headway. How could a church as prosperous as ours learn to trust God? Money from the sale of the old downtown property had made things too easy. We had paid $33,000 cash for thirty-three acres of new land in the suburbs. We had paid $25,000 cash for the lovely new parsonage and now still had over $30,000 remaining as a down payment on our new church building. No real faith or sacrifice had been called for to provide us with a new church.

"I almost wish something would happen which

would put us in a spot where we would *have* to trust God," I complained to Alice one night. "Our building program has just been too darned easy." A few weeks later my wish was granted.

Work was rapidly nearing completion on the church building, and the committee chosen to plan the services of dedication selected Sunday, December 8, as dedication day. With assurances from the contractor that all work would be completed at least three weeks prior to that date, the dedication programs were printed, special speakers secured and all plans finalized. But as the days passed, various delays slowed the construction and it became apparent the contractor would have to race against time to finish by the day of dedication. Our people began to feel uneasy.

December arrived and in a final flurry of activity the building itself was made ready for occupancy. But with dedication Sunday only a week away, all the final grading and paving of the lengthy driveway and parking lot remained to be done, and neither the paving contractor nor any of his equipment had yet appeared at the site.

"It will only take him two—maybe three days, once he's on the job," the building foreman assured me on Monday. "One day for grading and another day or so for paving."

But Tuesday morning brought with it a cold, sullen rain. All day Tuesday and Wednesday the rain fell, turning the ground surrounding the church into a sea of mud. Wednesday night the dedication committee met at the old tavern in emergency session in an attempt to decide upon some course of action. The gloomy weather outside was fully matched by the spirits of the committee members. Some immediately went on record for postponing the dedication service. Others suggested darkly that we should sue the paving contractor. Nearly all were agreed that it would be sheer folly to try to go ahead in the face of that expanse of mud.

"No one can get within a hundred yards of the

church without sinking up to his knees!" thundered one irate deacon.

"If we try to go ahead our church will be the laughing stock of Washington, D.C.," said another.

"Yes, but all the programs are printed and our services have been announced to all the other churches," reminded a third. On and on the discussion went, accompanied by the disheartening sound of rain, which seemed to be pelting all the harder against the windows.

Finally, one member asked for a chance to speak. "We're just wasting words and risking hurt feelings by going on like this. What has happened is nobody's fault. We can't help the weather. It seems to me this is one of those times when we simply have to trust God. Isn't that what you've been saying in your sermons, preacher?" Surprised and gratified by the turn of the conversation, I nodded.

The speaker went on. "Now, the Good Lord knows what our hopes and plans are. We claim to be building *His* church on property that has already been dedicated to *Him*, mud and all. Why don't we stop right now and lift this whole matter up to Him in prayer and let *Him* worry about the mud and the church's reputation?"

Since there seemed little other alternative, the committee agreed, and I was asked to lead in prayer. As we prayed I could sense an air of quiet relinquishment on the part of the committee members, and the meeting was adjourned with the Sunday dedication service still scheduled. We filed out into the rainy night without additional comment. Back at the parsonage I told Alice, "Looks like we've finally come to a situation where our people will have to trust God for a small miracle."

Thursday morning it was still raining. In the early afternoon I stood in the doorway of the church, talking to the building foreman.

"Isn't this one glorious mess? Here we are with a dedication service Sunday and a pre-dedication prayer service for our own people Saturday night and just look!"

I motioned at the mud. "Do you suppose we could lay a board walk from the highway to the church door?"

The foreman smiled. "I just spoke to the paving contractor on the telephone a minute ago. He's on his way out now to look things over. Why don't you wait around and see what he thinks about the situation?"

Minutes later the man arrived, and leaving his car parked by the highway, he came slogging up the hill through the mud to where we stood. After a brief conversation he spoke the first hopeful words I had heard all week.

"Weather forecast calls for clearing tonight. If there's no rain tomorrow we may be able to grade things into shape for blacktopping on Saturday."

Looking at the sloppy mess surrounding us I doubted it. "You mean you can grade the road and parking lot area tomorrow? But that's *mud!* How can you grade that stuff?" My incredulity didn't faze him. With a sweep of his arm he explained.

"All this paving area slopes, see? Most of the water will run off during the night if the rain stops. What's left we'll squeeze out tomorrow with bulldozers and rollers. This whole hill is pure bank gravel. It'll pack just fine."

But as if to mock his words, the rain began to rattle down all the harder, and I gazed in dismay at ten thousand tiny rivers coursing their way down across the bare sloping area where the road and parking lot had been marked off with wooden stakes. "Doesn't seem possible," I muttered. Still, I had to admit we had turned the whole muddy mess over to God in prayer.

Friday morning dawned dark and foreboding, with heavy rain clouds hovering just above the treetops. It looked as though the skies would tear open any minute and douse us with a fresh deluge. But the rains never came. All day long the bulldozers scraped and smoothed and the heavy motorized rollers pressed and squeezed dry the road and parking area. It was almost dark when they finished.

93

"We'll start paving at sun-up," the contractor told me, "and with luck we'll be through by six p.m."

I nodded dubiously. What was required was a driveway 16 feet wide and over four hundred feet long, two hundred feet from the highway entrance up alongside the church, and turning behind it another two hundred feet to the parsonage; plus a parking lot large enough for fifty cars. That would take a lot of asphalt.

I awoke at sun-up the next morning to the sound of heavy machinery outside the bedroom window. Peering out I was surprised to find the work begun. The first truck-load of smoking asphalt had just been dumped into the mechanized spreader as it began to inch its way from beside the parsonage toward the church, leaving a smoking black trail eight feet wide and six inches thick behind it. Down at the highway entrance I could see another half-dozen trucks parked, patiently waiting their turn to back up to the spreader and dump their cargoes.

All day long the trucks and crews swarmed around the spreader, and as the hours passed the solid black ribbon grew in length. As the spreader moved forward, men behind it with rakes smoothed the edges of the spread asphalt, making sure the borders of the road were even. Behind them shuttled two huge mechanized rollers, their fat steel wheels constantly bathed with tiny streams of water, pressing the asphalt hard and smooth with tons of pressure.

The weather was clear and bitter cold. I couldn't help thinking that even without the black-top we could have held the dedication services, for the near-zero weather had frozen the hillside solid. It was after sundown when the final load of asphalt was spread and rolled. A few minutes later the paving contractor joined me on the church steps. "There's your paving, preacher," he smiled, "just like I promised. Thanks to the cold weather you can drive on it right now. If it had been a warm day you couldn't have driven on it until tomorrow."

Twenty minutes later the first carloads of church members began arriving for the prayer service. Our people had dared to trust God and had not been disappointed.

CHAPTER THIRTEEN

Through the Shadowed Valley

ONE PARTICULAR AREA of the Christian ministry finds the young preacher at a decided disadvantage; that of pastoring the bereaved. The mystery of death defies pat answers, and the young minister, both by his youth and sheer inexperience, feels understandably inadequate.

The small church at Burkburnett where I pastored as a student had its share of deaths, and I soon acquired enough experience to conduct the funeral service itself without difficulty. But bringing real comfort and consolation to the grief-stricken family proved something else. As I sought to assure the bereaved of God's love and concern for them, I was always painfully aware that my own life had been singularly free from personal tragedy and grief.

I remember the gentle but humiliating rebuke I received at the hands of a tiny wisp of a widow, bowed by grief over the loss of her husband. In response to my glib words of comfort, she leaned over and patted me on the knee, and in a voice breaking with heartache murmured, "I know you mean well, Reverend, but you're so young—too young to know what I feel." I sat there glum with misery and fidgeting uncomfortably, admitting to myself that what she said was true. From that time on I made a determined effort to say less and pray more in my attempts to minister at the time of death.

At every funeral I found myself remembering the courageous and Spirit-filled testimony of Sybil Mae Archer and knew, deep within, that the spiritual resources she had called upon in her sudden grief were available for every Christian. Yet, somehow, so few church members seemed adequately prepared to face the experience of death. Secretly I wondered how I would measure up when the time eventually came for death to visit my immediate family. Would the sustaining love and comfort of the Holy Spirit see *me* through the trial, as I so confidently assured others He would? No one knows for certain until he faces such a time, and for each of us, personal exemption from life's ultimate experience is only temporary.

In the autumn of 1958, nearly two years after our ministry in Washington, D.C., began, Alice became pregnant with our fourth child. From the beginning—although she was never seriously ill—this pregnancy seemed different. The baby was due late in May, and as spring approached we were caught up in the busy schedule of church activities leading up to Holy Week and Easter. The days flew past and Alice, growing slow and clumsy as she approached her seventh month, suffered from increasing weariness. One day as we sat at the breakfast table she glanced at the calendar on the wall and sighed.

"Just two more months . . . if I can hang on to this baby that long."

Startled, I dropped my fork. "What do you mean, *'if* you can hang on to the baby that long'? Don't you feel well?"

"Oh, I feel well enough, I guess. It's just that . . . well . . . something seems different this time." Then she laughed and shrugged. "Just a case of nerves, I guess."

The chain of events which ushered us into the most tragic and yet the most glorious experience of our lives began, significantly enough, on Good Friday. There seemed to be something mystical and foreboding about the day itself. At noon I participated in the early minutes of a three-hour devotional service at the National City Christian Church in downtown Washington and then hurried back to my own church to baptize a teen-age girl who could not be present for our regular Easter Sunday baptismal service. That lovely and private ritual, with only the girl and her parents present, was concluded near 3 p.m., the traditional hour of Jesus' crucifixion.

We stepped outside the church afterward to find the daylight almost obliterated by a sky full of unbelievably dark clouds. It was as though the elements themselves had somehow conspired to commemorate, in a most startling and graphic manner, that terrible hour. We later learned that numbers of people downtown, fearing something more than coincidence in the sudden 3 p.m. darkness, left jobs and offices to rush home to be with their families.

The strange, oppressive atmosphere prevailed into the evening. Even our children seemed unusually quiet, and we all retired early. Sometime near midnight Alice woke me, saying in a strained voice, "Don, you'd better call the doctor. I'm afraid the baby's started to come."

The doctor's voice over the telephone was quiet and reassuring, but his words were not. "Drive Alice to the hospital and check her in. I don't know yet what this means, but we'd better be on the safe side. I'll call and tell them to be looking for you, and I'll be there as soon as I can, myself."

Calling on a neighbor to come in and stay with our children, I drove Alice to the hospital. As we slipped through the silent streets, Alice gently clasped my hand in hers.

"Honey, I know everything will be all right, for we'll have the Lord with us every minute." Even as she spoke, a measure of silent assurance seemed to flood the car.

By late Saturday morning the tests were complete and Alice's doctor came to the room to explain the gravity of the situation.

"There's no easy way to tell you this, but I know the two of you are strong enough to take it. Alice, there's no chance for your baby to be born normally. Our tests have confirmed that you have a condition known as 'placenta previa' which simply means that by some freakish accident the placenta has slipped beneath the baby and is blocking the birth canal. The only course open for us is to take the baby now, by Caesarean section."

The doctor paused, drew in a deep breath and continued, "The chances of the baby's survival are not good. After all, it will be two months premature. Could it be born in the normal way its chances would be vastly improved. But with surgery the shock will be so severe—well, all we can do is hope . . . and pray," he added belatedly, looking at me.

After he had gone Alice and I stared at each other wordlessly for a minute. I sat on the edge of the bed and drew her close to me. "It's still going to be all right, dear," she said, her voice muffled against my shoulder. Together we turned to Him in prayer.

The surgery was over so quickly, I was startled when the doctor entered the waiting room, still garbed in his surgical attire.

"Well, Don, you have a baby daughter."

"How's Alice?"

"Fine. She came through the surgery wonderfully well."

"And the baby?"

The faintest shadow appeared behind his eyes. "She's doing as well as could be expected under the circumstances, but it's too soon to tell anything. I suggest you call Alice's pediatrician right away."

I thanked the doctor and hurried to the telephone and called the pediatrician, who promised to come to the hospital immediately. Then I walked down to the nursery to ask if I could see the baby. A nurse wearing a surgical mask removed her from her isolette and brought her to the window. I had only a few seconds to peek at the tiny figure almost hidden in the nurse's arms. She was a half-sized living replica of her sisters and brother, early-struck from the same mold which had produced them, yet with such a shy, uncertain grip on this life. Silently I wondered, "Oh Lord, has life been granted this precious little form only to be taken away again?" I simply could not reconcile the thought with my belief in a loving Heavenly Father.

After a brief visit with Alice, I returned to the parsonage and told the other children all that had happened.

"We just have to wait and see if baby Holly gets to stay here. She's awfully tiny; maybe too tiny to come and live with us." The children seemed satisfied with my explanation.

Soon the pediatrician called and in brusque professional tones informed me she had examined the baby carefully. The major problem was—as with most "preemies"—a respiratory one. "It's too soon to tell if her lungs will develop sufficiently to enable her to overcome her breathing difficulty," she said, and then her tone softened perceptibly. "At this point I am not too hopeful, Mr. Basham."

The rest of the day I moved about in a mood of strange suspension, almost insulated from hope or any other feeling. I busied myself in caring for the children and in putting the finishing touches on my Easter sermon. I kept remembering that these were the hours between the Lord's death and His resurrection—a strangely-poised moment in history, a pause in the Divine-human encounter when both earth and heaven seemed to be holding their breaths, as if the issue between life and death were in doubt. By a strange combination of circumstances, Alice and I and little Holly were caught in that moment.

After a brief but poignant visit with Alice that night —a visit during which we agreed that no matter what happened, my proper place was in the pulpit on Easter morning—I returned to the parsonage and crawled wearily into bed. I was still asleep when the telephone rang at 7:00 a.m. the next morning. It was the pediatrician, and my heart sank as she spoke.

"I've just seen your baby. Her breathing difficulty has greatly increased during the night and she's losing ground. I'm afraid it's only a matter of hours now. You should come to the hospital as soon as possible."

My careful explanation of our decision that I should conduct the Easter service before coming to the hospital met with a long disapproving silence over the telephone. "Well, if that's what you've decided," the pediatrician finally spoke. "But don't expect me to comfort your wife. I must stay with the baby." And she hung up abruptly. It was clear she felt I should be with Alice, and in a way she was absolutely right. Still, our decision that I preach had been made, in part at least, out of a total commitment of little Holly's life back into the hands of God. I was determined to act in the light of that commitment.

The world outside gave no indication of our personal struggle. The day was alive with the glory of Easter. The church building and grounds were bathed in warm sunlight and the woods behind the church pealed with the sound of singing birds. Native redbud was in rampant bloom, splashing its purple color at random among trees as yet displaying only a grace edge of green. Wild dogwood blossomed in profusion throgh the woods, leaving white layers of blossoms floating like miniature snowstorms among their branches.

Walking from the parsonage to the church, surrounded by the beauty of that perfect morning, I breathed a fervent prayer. "Oh, God, let little Holly live! How can anything die in the midst of all this budding life?"

The service that Easter morning was alive with the presence of God, even from the opening strains of "Christ The Lord Is Risen Today". The church was jammed to overflowing, and the chancel beautifully decorated with white lilies whose perfume filled the air like incense. The choir sang with voices attuned to heaven, and when I rose to speak, I faced an audience made sensitive, not only by the magic of Easter, but by heartfelt sympathy for the struggle our family was enduring.

My text was the 20th chapter of John. I described how after the resurrection, Jesus gave each sorrowing

101

group of disciples all the proof they needed to believe that He had conquered death and was triumphantly alive. Those disciples were like us, I said, each at a different level of faith and understanding—and to each Jesus offered the evidence of His victory. Beginning with John, who believed when he saw the empty tomb; then to Mary, who believed when she heard the Lord call her by name; then to the disciples in hiding, to whom He miraculously appeared through closed doors; and at last to doubting Thomas, who would not believe until he saw the nailprints in Jesus' hands. To each yearning, hoping disciple Jesus gloriously revealed Himself and gave shining proof of His triumph over death.

During the sermon I became aware in some mystical way of the presence of little Holly, of Alice and of the Living Christ, and as the message reached its climax I was overwhelmed with the assurance of our personal immortality, and that the implications of our salvation in Jesus are far more glorious than we've dared to believe. In that moment I *knew* that all of us—Alice, me, little Holly, the other children, the members of the congregation, all who are linked to Christ—are a part of the very life of God Himself, a Life which is undefeatable, glorious and unending! I felt with unmistakable certainty that the crisis was over and that little Holly was safe—that we were all safe. Immersed in God as we are, nothing could ever really harm us. Those were moments of sheerest praise in which I could ask God for nothing and thank Him for everything.

At the close of the worship service, I rushed back to the house and telephoned the hospital.

"I was on my way to the telephone when you called, Mr. Basham," the pediatrician said quietly. "Your baby daughter died at ten minutes to twelve. I'm sorry. We did all we could."

The shock of her words turned my spine to jelly. I hung up the phone and sank into a chair nearby. *Little Holly dead?* For a minute I could not accept what the doctor said. "Your baby daughter died . . . I'm sorry."

How could it be? Just minutes before I had been so sure everything was all right—*so* sure!

Our two girls, Cindy and Sharon, gathered around my chair as Glenn, our two-year-old, clambered wide-eyed and innocent into my lap. With my arms around the three of them, I explained in halting words how little Holly had gone back to Heaven to live and would not be coming to stay with us. Cindy, the oldest, sensing my sudden grief, put her arms around my neck and in words poignantly similar to those her mother had spoken only hours before said, "It's going to be all right, Daddy. Jesus will take care of us. You'll see."

Leaving the children with a thoughtful deaconess who had come to the parsonage to offer assistance, I climbed in the car and drove toward the hospital. Half-blinded by tears, I began to pour out my grief in prayer to God. I was hurt and confused. "Oh, Lord, how could this happen after the assurance—the absolute assurance I felt during the morning service?" Suddenly, I was again ushered into that realm of understanding I had entered during the last minutes of my sermon. Once again the assurance of God's love swept over me and I was surrounded with an indescribable sense of security. "It *is* true," I found myself saying, "we *are* safe. All of us—and most of all—little Holly!"

I entered Alice's room at the hospital praying for the right words with which to break the news, but I didn't have to say anything. Tears filled her eyes as I knelt beside her bed.

"I am sorry, dearest. Everything humanly possible was done, but . . ." I couldn't go on. Alice reached out and put her arms around my neck.

"I know, I know . . . even the time it happened." She pushed me away for a moment and looked into my eyes. "It was just before noon, wasn't it?" I nodded.

"I knew it," she continued. "All morning I felt so close to her, and to you, and to Jesus. Then a few minutes before twelve there came this great sense of peace; the feeling that everything was all right. Nobody would

103

tell me, but I knew then she had gone . . . no, not gone," Alice paused, searching for a better word. Then, smiling through her tears, she said, "Gone *home*."

The days which followed were filled with the constant miracle of God's gentle comforting presence. As any parents losing a child, we grieved deeply, but there was no bitterness. Our grief seemed transformed into something beyond sorrow by a Holy Presence so real and reassuring that it more than matched our sense of loss. Every time the cold fear of death threatened to break in on us, it was dispelled by the warmth of God's love enfolding and sheltering us, a love so vital and living it simply denied death. It was so real that we often found ourselves giving comfort to those who came seeking to comfort us.

Alice's recovery was astonishing, and the following Friday, just one week after she had been admitted to the hospital, I brought her home. Sensing her hunger to see and hold the children, I brought them with me in the car. Our reunion was a profound and tender one, and we drove away from the hospital with the children sitting as close to their mother as they could. The day was fully as beautiful as Easter Sunday had been, and as we drove through the morning sunlight past the Potomac Tidal Basin, the famed Japanese cherry trees were blooming in their full blaze of splendor.

But the beauty outside was no more wondrous than the joy and love we shared there in the privacy of our car. The Holy Spirit seemed to rejoice in our reunion, as human and Divine love mingled and flowed together. We knew that the visitation of that tiny precious life, which had paused so briefly in its eternal journey to grace our lives—just twenty-four hours—had somehow drawn us closer to one another and to the Lord than we had ever been before.

Little Sharon expressed it with the wisdom given only to the very young when she said happily, "Now there's really *four* of us children, isn't there, Mother? Except one is staying in Heaven with Jesus."

Alice hugged Sharon to her and turned to me with that joy born out of suffering diffusing her lovely face.

"The greatest miracle of all," she said, "is that with Jesus, even when you lose, you win."

CHAPTER FOURTEEN

If You Can't Do It Here . . .

AFTER NEARLY FIVE YEARS at the church in Washington, D.C., I came to the firm conviction that I should seek another pastorate. While there had been the few mountain-peaks of spiritual experience which reminded us of God's hand on our lives, nevertheless the outward growth of the church had been too easy and the inner growth too slight for me to be content. In deep disappointment I admitted my failure in opening the way for a ministry of the Holy Spirit in that congregation. Instead of leading the people down the path of spiritual depth and blessing, I seemed to be conforming more and more to the image of complacent pastor, popular preacher and community leader. I felt it was necessary to flee that easy "success", partly for my own soul's welfare, so when a call came from the Hillcrest Christian Church in Toronto, Canada, I jumped at the chance.

Hillcrest was a decided contrast to the fast-growing congregation we left behind. A sophisticated congregation with a country-club atmosphere, it had been carefully cultivated through the years as the church of some of Toronto's leading citizens. However, it was now well-past its prime years, and being located in the inner city, it ministered largely on past momentum. All the problems inner-city churches face were evident—a declining membership in a rapidly-changing and deteriorating neighborhood, and a widely-scattered membership which commuted for miles to come together for worship. The church no longer had any real identification with, nor ministry to, the neighborhood surrounding it. Still capable of gathering a sizeable congregation and maintaining a substantial yearly budget, it was comprised of cheerful, successful families who, while realizing the church was on the decline, were nonetheless satisfied with the status quo.

Stung by a sense of spiritual failure in my former ministry, at Hillcrest I began with my very first sermon to preach not only the need for a personal, saving relationship with Jesus Christ, but also for discipline in a life of prayer and for the power of the Holy Spirit.

The people gave token approval to the vigor of my preaching, admired my personal convictions, spoke vaguely about this being "what the church needs, all right", and *did nothing*. In spite of my determination to bear down on the great central themes of the Christian faith, almost a year passed with no evidence of any kind of spiritual break-through. In fact my sustained emphasis on sermons about spiritual power and the need for personal, spiritual discipline tended to alienate a portion of the congregation. "The new minister takes his religion too seriously," some said.

But while I was reluctant to admit it, deep down I knew the reason why my ministry didn't seem to be getting anywhere. It was because I kept skirting around the reality of my own experience. I was quick to point out what the Holy Spirit was doing in other lives and other churches but remained tactfully silent about His power in my own life. Apparently the Lord grew tired of my procrastination, for He began dealing with me over my reluctance to give my own personal testimony to the fullness of His power as I had personally experienced it—including tongues.

"Tongues, Lord? Witness to the baptism and tongues in a sophisticated church like Hillcrest?" I tried to rationalize, but the Lord seemed adamant. As I continued to procrastinate, one day it struck me with terrifying clarity: "If Jesus Christ were to return today, how could I justify my reluctance to proclaim what He had done in my life?" I suddenly recalled the wise counsel of Rufus

Moseley, that without a faithful witness to the power of the Holy Spirit my ministry would be robbed of power. Rufus had planned to write another book—one which he never finished—to be called, *Receiving the Full Salvation; Bearing the Full Testimony*. That title haunted me. I knew I had received "the full salvation"; I also knew I was not "bearing the full testimony". But still I hesitated. Suppose I told them and they didn't believe me—what then? If only I could be sure people would receive my testimony sympathetically. But I could not be sure.

As I had often done in the past, I poured out my feelings in a letter to a trusted friend, Dr. G. Edwin Osborn, then head of the Department of Practical Theology at Phillips University. A gentle, sensitive soul who was a recognized author and leader among the Disciples of Christ in the fields of worship and the devotional life, Dr. Osborn had been a great source of inspiration during my seminary years. More than any other professor he understood and encouraged my spiritual quest, and at times his wise and loving counsel had helped me through dreary periods of frustration and spiritual barrenness. His reply to my letter of self-pity and bitter complaint over the spiritual indifference of Christendom at large and my own congregation in particular, was one of compassion and understanding.

Dear Don,

How I love you! For your witness, your concern, your prayers, your devotion. Perhaps I should also include, for your agony of spirit as you crave for others of us, and for your brethren, the same richness of spiritual experience you know. God will not let your efforts go unattended, even though He may fulfill your intense desire in some other way than you now even dream of—but cling to your hope and God will use you.

I'm grateful for the warming of my own experience and the enriching of my witness by your faithfulness. I have not yet experienced the kind of manifestation of the Spirit that you have, but I do not resist it. I seek to give the Spirit

108

full sweep in my life. I try to help my students understand that you cannot bind God in our human-made molds—if we try it, He breaks out in unexpected places.

I do rejoice in the widening expanse of the Spirit's influence in our church life. I think, were you to drop in at University Place Church here, you could feel the difference.

Don, you chafe under the resistance of many of your leaders—and that is human—but you are of the Spirit, and *patience* is one of the fruits of the Spirit. God doesn't hold you responsible for their spiritual baptism; He attends to that so long as you are faithful in your witness. Don't push yourself out of a position where you can witness, for then God would have to raise up someone else to be the channel of interpretation for them.

Someday—soon or far distant—a church will allow God to break through and it will be like a light, or a city on a hill. I do not want you to silence your witness—demonstrate it! I do not want you to destroy your witness either; but continue to dedicate it to the use of God's Spirit; He is in charge. Meanwhile, keep writing and please know what a spiritual help you are to me in your newsletters. You don't know how far-reaching that work will be. Do you suppose Paul ever dreamed of the earthshaking results of his letters? And know my love for you.

Sincerely,
G. Edwin Osborn

"I do not want you to silence your witness . . ." Under the prompting of the Holy Spirit, this simple statement in Dr. Osborn's letter became a command. In earlier correspondence he had suggested that I write out my experience and beliefs so as to share them with others. Now, I felt assured the time had come. Reluctantly at first, then with increasing enthusiasm, I set to work and prepared a 25-page manuscript of my testimony. I then began circulating it in mimeographed form to those I knew would be interested. Spirit-filled friends across the country welcomed an added testimony to their own, and I had soon distributed nearly 200 copies of the report.

Wanting to be completely open and above board

about what I was doing, I gave a copy to each member of my board of elders, asking each in turn to read it carefully and comment on it at our next meeting. The elders did just that, and the meeting the following month was one I shall not soon forget.

After some polite initial comment, the boom was lowered. The board of elders quickly made it plain that they felt I had really gone off the deep end. Pointed references to the danger of splitting the church, the possible loss of income, the need for refraining from introducing any teaching or practice which might be considered controversial, all were brought to my attention. While the elders took no official action either to condemn the report or to prevent further circulation of it, nevertheless by the time the meeting concluded, they had left no doubt where they stood. I had been rebuked and chastised as an erring child.

One of the elders, himself an ordained minister, took pains after the meeting to warn me of the grave dangers of "this kind of fanaticism". He pointed out that my testimony in no way described a "normative Christian experience", quoting the old argument that since Jesus had not spoken in tongues, there was no reason for us to either.

"I hope you will not be foolish enough to endanger your ministry further by continuing to advocate and support a doctrine and practice so foreign to the Disciples of Christ," he concluded.

Another elder, one of Canada's leading businessmen, mentioned that he had passed his copy of the testimony on to one of the senior members of the congregation, an elderly trustee, much loved and admired, who read only the first few pages and became so angry that he returned the copy. He had not been in church since.

"I suggest you get in touch with him, Don, and see if you can mend some fences." This elder had then sent the testimony to a close personal friend, J. Irwin Miller, who at that time was serving as president of the National

110

Council of Churches. I never learned Miller's reaction to it.

I left the elders' meeting realizing that while the door might not have been entirely slammed shut against witnessing to the baptism in the Holy Spirit at Hillcrest, any such witness would prove difficult, and I could count on no help or support from any of my elders. I would have to go it alone.

The next day I got in touch with the offended trustee and arranged to have lunch with him at his club. Afterward we sat and talked the better part of the afternoon. At first our discussion was as awkward for him as for me. Determined to be frank, he went down a carefully prepared list of things he objected to in my preaching. He was fully convinced I had no right, as a minister in a Disciple church, to preach what he called "heretical doctrine". I soon discovered that by heretical doctrine he meant my frequent mention of the power of prayer, of the supernatural elements of our Christian faith and especially any mention of the current outpouring of the Holy Spirit.

He went on to say that one Sunday, when he had friends in church, I made mention in my sermon of the church's recovery of the ministry of spiritual healing. After the service he had felt obliged to apologize to his friends for my fanaticism. Then, there were other occasions when I preached on matters which were "highly improper" for the minister of Hillcrest to deal with. "After all, you have a certain image which must be maintained," he insisted.

As the discussion continued, we became more frank and open with one another. I had prayed fervently before the appointment that anything I said would be both loving and uncompromising. I shared my deep concern over the spiritual indifference of many church members and my determination to be a faithful witness to what God is doing in our day. I noticed that his attitude began to soften. I then gently rebuked him for not having

111

shown me the courtesy of finishing the entire testimony I had written before rejecting its thesis.

"Perhaps I did act a bit hastily," he admitted.

"Then are you willing to read the whole report now?"

He smiled and shook his head. "I don't think that would do any good. You and I are just too far apart in what we believe."

I asked him to share some of his beliefs with me and found his theology bordering on a kind of benevolent religious humanism. He had long ago rejected the miracle stories in the Scriptures, freely admitting that such doctrines as the virgin birth of Christ seemed childish if not sheer nonsense. Using his arguments as ammunition, I pressed home my conviction that a minister of the Gospel has the responsibility to preach only what he really believes.

"Do you realize you have just shared with me a theology which at least 75 of our church members would reject as totally untenable? The views you hold are more contrary to our church's historic position than are mine, yet you consider yourself a good Disciple and a sincere Christian. And no one denies you the right to share your convictions. Allow me the same privilege."

He looked thoughtfully at me for several seconds and then said with a faint trace of a smile, "I suppose I really shouldn't be too critical when you preach about the power of prayer. Even though I'm not really sure I believe in it, nevertheless I've seen it work in my own life."

Then he related an incident which had happened some years before, while he and his wife were on a prolonged tour of Europe. She became seriously ill; and in that strange land, with only the services of a doctor whose language he could not speak, he became fearful almost to the point of despondency.

"I didn't know which way to turn," he said. "Should I abandon the tour and rush my wife home for treatment? And if I did, could she stand the trip? Yet I had no confidence that the doctor treating her was really competent. I had no one to turn to for advice, so one morning I slipped into an old historic chapel near our hotel. We had visited it a few days before as tourists—now I came to pray. And I know God heard me. It seemed as if He spoke to me, telling me not to be afraid and assuring me my wife would soon recover and that we would continue our tour. And that's just the way things worked out."

He finished in a voice shaky with emotion, "I've never told that story to a living soul, not even my wife."

I didn't know what to say next. I had been all set to criticize his theology, which was so unscriptural it made me wince, only to be cut short by this deeply moving witness.

"Well, I can't agree with your theology," I said, "but I certainly can say 'Amen!' to your testimony." We parted amiably, and he was in church the following Sunday.

Among the first persons to receive a copy of the mimeographed testimony was Dr. Osborn at Phillips University. I knew he was serving as a member of a study committee under the auspices of the World Convention of Churches of Christ, whose topic was "The Nature and Work of the Holy Spirit". He seemed delighted to receive my report, and his heart-warming response helped to offset the critical reaction of my own elders.

Dear Don,

Thank you beyond measure for your paper, *Adventure In Pentecost*. The document came last Monday by special delivery in time for our Tuesday meeting.

I do not know how adequately to thank you, or to tell you how greatly I was moved by my reading of it Monday night. It made a similar impression on the Study committee to whom I read it Tuesday afternoon. Needless to say, the members did not accept it instantly, but no one rejected its message, and in its discussion all felt that here is a place for further study and that the Disciples need to give the matter further consideration.

My own reaction has been one of openness to the

leading of God. I have tried to make myself receptive to Him in whatever way He may care to use me. That has been my sincere prayer for more than a quarter of a century. I have never had the experience of speaking with tongues—honestly, I have not sought it. I think on at least one occasion, perhaps several more, the Holy Spirit has used me in a healing ministry. Maybe I am too hesitant to make much of this. I do not think it is reluctance, however. I feel sure it isn't. But I have always felt the Spirit would take the initiative, when a heart is open to Him.

A paper I read to the group on the Holy Spirit and Worship is being mimeographed. When ready, I'll send you a copy. I am keeping a copy of your paper; the other was left with the committee's drafting group at their request.

Please write me again, and keep me in your prayers that God may find in me an instrument for His use, or as you so beautifully put it in your paper, a vessel for his precious treasure.

My warm greetings to Alice and the children, and my abiding affection.

Sincerely,
G. Edwin Osborn

Shortly afterwards, the same guidance of the Holy Spirit which led me to circulate the testimony also moved me to prepare a sermon dealing directly with the subject and with my own experience. Fully expecting a critical reaction to the sermon, I spent much of the Saturday night before the fateful morning of its delivery in prayer.

I followed the choir into the sanctuary that Sunday morning with fear and trembling. Though determined to be faithful to the guidance I had received, I felt like a lamb being led to the slaughter. What course of action should I follow if real controversy were to ensue? Suppose they asked me to resign? Taking my place in the pulpit chair, I sought comfort in the familiar surroundings—the dark, rich panelling of the chancel walls, the soft gleam of polished communion ware, the lofty stained-glass window above the baptistry, the familiar sea of faces in the congregation—but none of these helped. Twice during the early minutes of the service I was tempted to toss aside my sermon outline and revert to an earnest-sounding but inoffensive message which would make the congregation smile and nod their heads.

Finally it was time to preach. I stood up behind the pulpit, breathed a silent prayer for the Holy Spirit to use me and began to speak. I had not spoken a half-dozen sentences before I knew it would be uphill all the way. I have known Sundays when my congregation drew insight and wisdom from me I didn't know I possessed. But that Sunday it was as if I were a complete stranger to them and they were complete strangers to me. So far as I could detect, there was not a flicker of response or reaction to anything I said.

With a strange numbness I finished the message and, following the benediction, took my place at the door, braced for critical comment. To my astonishment, there was none. The congregation filed past the door shaking my hand as usual, smiling the same impersonal smiles and making the same impersonal comments I had heard a hundred times before. "Nice service, pastor." "Enjoyed your message, Reverend." "Nice to be in church today, pastor."

" 'Nice service,' you say? 'Enjoyed the message,' you say? What's the matter with you people?" I screamed back at them silently, a bleak smile frozen on my face. "What does it take to move you? Can't you see what that sermon cost me? Didn't you see it dripping with my life's blood?"

I shut the doors against the back of the last departing worshipper and headed through the church toward my study blinking back tears. I felt like every member who had shaken my hand had stepped on me. All that prayer, all that effort, all that wrestling against fear . . . and for what? For *nothing!* Either no one had understood what I said, which would have been bad enough, or else they understood and just didn't care, which was worse. I had been prepared to suffer criticism and rebuke for the Lord's sake, but I wasn't even granted the courtesy of a reaction. Even the elders' meeting hadn't been that bad. Surely I had misinterpreted my guidance. To be rebuked is painful, but to be ignored is humiliating!

Some days later as I drove home from an out-of-town meeting, still puzzled and hurt over the indifference of the congregation to my testimony, I began pouring out my feelings in prayer to God. As I prayed, I was suddenly seized with a great, compassionate sadness for the church. Tears welled up in my eyes as my prayer switched over into unknown tongues, and I felt the Holy Spirit begin to share my burden. Then, in response to my prayer came a silent Voice, "I have heard your prayers and have seen your tears and say to you, take heart! Your ministry will yet bear fruit among the people. There are those numbered in your midst upon whom I shall pour out My Spirit, for I have many people in your city."

I rejoiced at this comforting prophecy and felt strengthened and encouraged for a day or two. But soon my despondency returned and I rationalized the prophecy away, saying it was probably just wishful thinking on my part. Before long it dropped completely from my mind, not to be recalled until months after it was fulfilled.

Although some small comfort came with the knowledge that I had been faithful—at least in my witness in the sermon and the written testimony—nothing changed, and the months that followed proved the most difficult I have ever experienced in the ministry. Outwardly things went on as usual. I preached the Word, counselled the troubled, visited the sick, married the living and buried the dead as dutifully as before. But inwardly I was desolate.

Finally, I became so discouraged that Satan convinced me the situation was hopeless. If the kind of ministry I longed to render was not welcome, I would find another pulpit, back in the southwestern part of the United States where my wife and I had been reared and where we had friends and family. I justified my decision to myself saying, "People will surely be more responsive to the Holy Spirit back home." Besides, if I had to end up being a plain, powerless preacher doing plain, powerless things, at least I could do them in a part of the country where we were known and loved. I contacted our denominational headquarters asking that my name stand for relocation.

Then one day, soon after filing my request, I was sitting in my study at the church reading. Suddenly, the words seemed to leap from the page. Through them the Holy Spirit spoke to me with great authority. *"If you can't do it here, you can't do it anywhere."* I knew it was God, but somehow I was just too blue and discouraged to care. We would still move—just as soon as the right offer came.

But the right offer never came. The Lord, in His grace, closed all doors and kept them closed. The half dozen or so tentative offers I received were seeking personnel with interests and qualifications which I did not possess. The few letters of inquiry I sent got nowhere. I had reached a dead end and felt like a man condemned to die. The knowledge that unless we saw the Holy Spirit fall on Hillcrest church, we might never see Him fall anywhere, seemed too great a burden to bear. I felt we couldn't continue our ministry there, yet the Lord said we couldn't leave.

In deep despondency I wrote to Harald Bredesen, one of our close friends in the Holy Spirit who had ministered to us the night we had received the baptism in the Holy Spirit years before. His reply was like a ray of sunlight piercing the gloom.

Dear Don,
  Your lament from the wilderness has reached me here in Hawaii. Though this is a far cry from the wilderness, your letter certainly strikes some responsive chords. The description of the situation in your church sounds like an exact description of the one in my own, except for the fact that I do have a handful of people who have received the baptism. But for the most part the attitude of my people is the same as yours, or perhaps I should say, they are in

the next stage after yours—that is to say, they feel "this stuff is fine for those who want it but count me out".

During the preceding stage, when the going was very tough, I became so desperate that I spent whole nights in the church where I would be free to cry out to God without disturbing my wife. During that time my favorite prayer was, "Oh, Lord, it is enough now, take away my life." It seemed as if the irresistible force had met the immovable obstacle and there was no hope at all. Yet, it was during that furnace experience that God was battering me into shape for His use; it was preparation for this worldwide and very thrilling door of opportunity that God has opened to me now.

It seems strange that I should be going around the world as the visiting expert, helping many people of all denominations into this experience, while in a very real sense I have been, and am, a failure on my own front. Remember this though, dear brother Don, God is not so much interested in your success in your church as His success in *you!* Forget about the results you are having or not having and just concentrate on being God's man.

As you let Him make you that, one of two things will happen; either there will be a break in your church or God will lead you out to a place of larger opportunity. Many times the person who breaks the ice for the full Gospel in a given situation incurs such rancor that he cannot be used of God to usher in the new day. David was a man of war; he could not build the temple; he could only gather the material for it.

I pray that your very sense of frustration and desperation, which I know so well in my own experience, may be used of God to crowd you into real plaudit ministry wherein you may spend many hours each week in seeking His face in prayer and in His word. Be sure to exercise faithfully the gift of tongues, even when you don't feel edified, even when you don't see the results. Take it by faith—"He that speaks with an unknown tongue edifieth himself and speaks mysteries unto God".

Eternally in Christ,
Harald

The fact that sunlit peaks are joined by shadowed valleys is as true of the soul's journey as of the earth's

118

geography. But thankfully, our valleys of adversity and the temptation to flee, like Jonah, before God's will do not last too long. There comes an end to every trial. "God is faithful, and he will not let you be tempted beyond your strength, but with the temptation will also provide the way of escape, that you may be able to endure it" (I Cor. 10:13).

So it proved to be with us. In the midst of our agony of soul, God was at work. Yet the first evidence of the Holy Spirit's moving was to appear, not in Hillcrest Church, but in a member of my own family—a long, long way from Toronto.

CHAPTER FIFTEEN

Twelve Stone Steps to the Sky

IT BEGAN ONE MORNING when I received a letter from my brother, Hal, a colonel in the Air Force, who was stationed in Hawaii. Hal had followed the years of my spiritual quest with more than casual interest, and on occasion his own life had been touched by the power of God. Years before, when Alice and I first lived at the Koinonia Foundation in Baltimore, he had written us from Panama, where he was stationed, to request prayer for his wife. She had been admitted to the hospital after tests and X-rays revelaed she had tuberculosis.

We sent him some literature on healing and quickly enlisted all the people at Koinonia to pray for his wife. God heard and answered those prayers. A few days later we received a jubilant letter telling how the doctors, after further tests and X-rays, had decided that his wife didn't have tuberculosis after all. "The first series of tests and X-rays must have been taken improperly," they told him. Hal's letter also revealed how deeply his own life had been touched by God during the prayer vigil for his wife.

Now he was writing for help again. His wife had contracted arthritis in Hawaii and was being sent back to Texas to an Air Force hospital near her parents' home. Hal was to be reassigned to the base where she would be receiving treatment. He asked us to pray for his wife and for the host of problems arising from the emergency transfer. Next, his letter spoke wistfully of the need for the power of the Holy Spirit in his life, and finally he asked if there was any chance that I might be able to come to Texas in time for deer season. He felt

that the few days' leave he might have before beginning
his new assignment would enable him to make the annual hunt with our father, and he hoped I could join
them. I knew his interest in my coming was motivated
as much by his deep spiritual need as by the desire for
us to hunt together.

Praying over his letter, I felt strongly impressed that
if we could meet and pray, Hal would receive the baptism
in the Holy Spirit. I replied that I would meet him in
Texas if it were God's will.

Alice agreed I should go and, surprisingly, my
church board granted permission for the trip. So a few
weeks later, in mid-November, I found myself at Toronto's International Airport at dawn, boarding a plane
for Texas. In my pocket was a letter from Hal. He said
he had arrived in Texas from Hawaii just a few days before and found his wife comfortably settled and responding to treatment. Everything was set for the hunt.

As the plane headed south I watched the sun break
free of the horizon to sift its fingers through the morning haze, gilding the small lakes and ponds below and
dotting the drab landscape like shiny, silver coins scattered on a carpet. The lovely sight brought back memories of youthful days, when Hal and I had seen the sun
rise and set over such ponds as we roamed the Texas
prairies hunting ducks and geese. Some prairie landmarks were still as vivid in my mind as when I was a boy
of twelve; the bend in a certain pasture road, a creaky
windmill beside a corral, a single leaning cottonwood
tree and a rural church standing alone on a small rise
with twelve stone steps leading up to its door. I remembered the winter day we drove past to find the church
burned to the ground. Only the steps were left. The
church was never rebuilt, but the steps remained for
years afterward—like an unfinished altar. Twelve stone
steps to the sky, silently reminding us that buildings are
not essential for God to reveal Himself to man.

"... the Most High does not dwell in houses made
with hands, as the prophet says, 'Heaven is my throne

121

and earth is my footstool. What house will you build for me, says the Lord, or what is the place of my rest?" (Acts 7:48–49).

In our egotism we continue to erect lavish houses of worship, dedicating them to the glory of God but using them to impress and compete with one another, forgetting that God is not impressed with brick and mortar. When the disciples bragged about the architecture of the temple in Jerusalem, Jesus replied simply, "Truly, I say to you there will not be left here one stone upon another that shall not be thrown down" (Matt. 24:2).

In contrast, my flight to Texas was motivated by the conviction that it is within *man*, not within places, that God means to dwell. "Do you not know that *you* are the temple of God and that God's Spirit dwells in *you?*" (I Cor. 3:16). This was the discovery I knew awaited my brother once he was baptized in the Holy Spirit.

A layer of clouds drifted beneath the plane's wing to hide the earth from view. But as prayers and memories continued to mingle, I could see that in those years of growing up in the out-of-doors God had been trying to reveal Himself to my brother and me—through clean, cold winds, through sunrises and sunsets and through the calm distances of the prairies themselves. Something sacred can happen to a youngster when he stands alone on broad prairie pastures, knowing that he is taller than anything else for miles around. A portion of those quiet spaces comes stealing within and broadens the borders of his soul. But the revelation of God in nature is not enough, and my reverie ended as I fervently thanked God that neither He nor I, nor my brother, could rest content until that early revelation became personally redemptive and powerful through the Lord Jesus Christ and the Holy Spirit.

Hal met me in Wichita Falls, and the next day we drove with our father into the heart of south Texas to the James River Ranch, thirty miles west of the little town of Mason. For some the rugged beauty of that country has little appeal, but ten years had passed since I had seen it last, and it was a welcome sight to me. Thousands of square miles of low, rocky hills and plateaus covered with scrub cedar, oak, chapparal brush, mesquite and other thorny growth, most of it untouched and unchanged since the days when the Indians had it all to themselves. In fact, our camp along the Devil's River was located near an old Indian campground, and we often discovered arrow points and other Indian artifacts while hunting. Even today the land is good for little but ranching—supporting meager herds of white-faced cattle and angora goats. A vast, primitive area, it is a timeless haven for the elusive white-tailed deer.

The first three days were given totally to the companionship and joy of hunting, with no mention of the more basic reason for my coming. Our dad, although past seventy, is still an expert marksman, and so is Hal. My accuracy with a deer rifle is only fair, but by the end of the third day, I, too, had been successful and each of us had his first buck.

The fourth day dawned grey and rainy, and as I awoke to the sound of rain pelting the tent roof, I rejoiced inwardly, feeling certain this would be God's day.

After breakfast, Hal and I drove into town for supplies, and all the wet, thirty miles there and back we talked of the things of God. The rain was still pouring down, and we were singing hymns together as we turned through the pasture gate for the last mile back to camp. Then Hal suddenly turned the station wagon out of the narrow road and drove twenty yards into the brush and parked.

"Any reason why we can't pray for me right here?" he asked. There wasn't, so we began to pray.

I asked the Lord to fill him with the Holy Spirit and then began praying quietly in tongues. With his head leaning against his hands as he gripped the steering wheel, Hal humbly invited the Holy Spirit to come within and flood his life. Only a minute had passed be-

123

fore tears began coursing down his cheeks, and he opened his mouth and began praising God in an unknown tongue. God, who is always faithful, had granted his heart's desire!

A little later, Hal interrupted the flow of heavenly language and turned to me.

"What if I can't pray like this when I'm alone? Will you write down what it sounds like I'm saying, so I can look at it later if I need it?" I agreed and started to write down the words and syllables on the back of the grocery list we took to town. After a few lines I gave up and thrust the paper back in my pocket, for by then Hal was praying so freely in his new language of praise that I knew he would never need words written down on paper to confirm his receiving Jesus' baptism in the Holy Spirit.

Two days later I flew back to Toronto, and within a week I received a letter from Hal. He told me that before breaking camp, he returned to the place where we had prayed, gathered some stones and erected a small altar to mark the spot where God had blessed him. It was a touching and unusual act of reverence; but, then, my brother has never conformed to the usual image of a church member, and I doubt he ever will. Yet today he is a man who knows that the Spirit of God dwells in him, leading and guiding his life.

The landmarks of our hunting days are still as clear in my memory today; the bend in a certain pasture road, the creaky windmill beside a corral, the single, leaning cottonwood tree and those twelve stone steps to the sky. But, praise God, a *new* landmark has been added—a more significant pile of stones. For I know that in Mutton pasture on the James River Ranch, thirty miles west of Mason, Texas, at a spot known only to two men and God—and a few white-tailed deer—there stands one small altar erected to the glory of our Lord Jesus Christ, who still baptizes in the Holy Spirit.

". . . when your children ask in time to come, What do these stones mean to you? Then you shall tell them . . ."
(Joshua 4:6-7).

CHAPTER SIXTEEN

Signs and Wonders

NOT LONG AFTER my return to Toronto it became apparent that the Holy Spirit was finally beginning to move in the lives of a few of the Hillcrest members. Some of the seed we had sown had fallen on fertile soil, taken root and now were beginning to grow like corn in the night.

One Sunday after church a young couple to whom we had witnessed and for whom we had prayed—apparently without success—approached me with the news that they had attended a prayer meeting in a Pentecostal church and received the baptism in the Holy Spirit. I was grateful, yet secretly sad they had found it necessary to go to another church.

Shortly thereafter another couple, recently moved to Toronto, joined our church and quickly established themselves in the teaching ministry. They also had received the baptism in the Holy Spirit. I was delighted to have them but couldn't help reminding myself that they had found the experience somewhere else.

Then one snowy night in February, Rev. Byron Howlett, minister of the Disciple Church in Guelph, Ontario, accompanied me to a service in downtown Toronto where the Rev. Dennis Bennett, Spirit-filled Episcopalian priest from Seattle, Washington, addressed a huge crowd on the subject of the world-wide charismatic revival.

Byron knew first-hand the healing power of the Holy Spirit. Some years before, public attention had been focused on his small church when the prayers of the congregation resulted in the sudden healing of a parishioner who lay dying in the hospital. Area newspapers had picked up the story and given it wide publicity. But like many other devoted ministers, Byron sensed there was a dimension of spiritual power he had not yet penetrated. He was seeking more of God.

After the meeting, during which many of Byron's fears and questions about the baptism in the Holy Spirit had been resolved, we returned to the parsonage to pray. The Holy Spirit moved quickly and graciously in response to our prayers, and in a few minutes, Byron was filled with ι e Holy Spirit, rejoicing that God had moved with new power into his life. While we were praying, prophecy came, promising that although there would be censure for Christ's sake, nevertheless we were standing on the threshold of great signs and wonders which would accompany the outpouring of God's Holy Spirit upon our churches.

As we parted I felt marvelously clean and light, as if I were walking on air. Suddenly, I realized why. The heavy burden I had carried during those long months when I had resisted God's will and tried to leave the place He had appointed me to serve, had suddenly lifted. Struggling faith had burst through to *living* hope.

When three additional members in our church reported to me they had received the baptism in the Holy Spirit—not in ours, but other churches!—I knew it was time to form a prayer group. Confirmation of this was soon coming, for at the very first meeting everyone sensed that we were in the center of a Divine arrangement, and that our gathering would be a focal point for the release of great spiritual power. Through prophecy it was revealed that together we would manifest a much greater spiritual power than the sum total of our individual faiths, and that the Holy Spirit's presence in our midst would create the spiritual climate where all manner of signs and wonders could be brought forth to the honor of Christ's name.

One of the first evidences of the Holy Spirit's power

126

at work was the healing of a congenital eye defect in Stan Hopkins, who was serving as chairman of the church's administrative board. After prayer, his left eye —almost sightless and closed since birth—was wonderfully opened and the vision remarkably improved. The physical transformation was apparent to all who knew him and provided startling confirmation of his witness to how God had worked an even greater miracle in his heart and life through the baptism in the Holy Spirit. In a matter of months the Holy Spirit changed this man from a shy, uncertain church member into a vital, witnessing Christian who could testify and preach with power.

Next, a lovely Jamacan girl, Joyce, joined our group. She had spent years searching for certainty in her Christian life. Now she found it through the baptism in the Holy Spirit. The week following her baptism, she returned to the prayer meeting to tell how she had been repeatedly asked by fellow workers to explain the smiling radiance of her face.

One night a small group of us were gathered in the church parlor for prayer when a young couple came through the door, the wife hobbling in on crutches. Lilian was in great pain, suffering from the recurrence of a leg ailment which had previously resulted in lengthy hospitalization, followed by partial paralysis for some two years. The circulation was severely impaired, leaving the lower limb numb and useless. Even to touch her foot to the floor brought excruciating pain. Lilian and Brian had heard reports of the prayer group and came seeking help.

I confess that Lilian's obvious distress caused me to think panicky thoughts. Who were we to believe we could help her? I wished desperately for a moment that we had never gotten into the business of praying for people. Summoning my courage I suggested to Lilian that she sit in a large, comfortable chair near the center of the room. Painfully, she made her way to the chair and sat down, placing her crutches on the floor beside her. It was obvious that she was a little frightened and very ill at ease.

Gathering around her chair we prayed earnestly for the Lord to heal her, that His name might be glorified in our church. It was immediately apparent the Holy Spirit was present with power. After the prayer, Lilian looked up with a beaming smile.

"Why, the pain is gone," she said, "and such a sense of peace came over me when you prayed!" Then she confessed, "You don't know how difficult it was for me to come here and ask for prayer . . . and when you gathered around the chair to pray I was so frightened I wanted to get up and leave the room." Then she laughed, "But God made sure I couldn't—somebody was standing on my crutches!"

Even as Lilian spoke the circulation was being restored to her leg. Before the end of the meeting she could put weight on the foot and had discarded one crutch. In response to further prayer she and her husband both received the baptism in the Holy Spirit. The next morning she telephoned to say she had thrown away the other crutch and was completely healed. Sunday she and her husband were in church, simply glowing with physical and spiritual health.

Since many people had seen her hobbling about on crutches, her healing greatly stirred the congregation. But to Lilian, the miracle of her physical healing was only a part of the greater transformation wrought in her life by the abiding presence of the Holy Spirit. Yet, ironically enough, she found that many of the people with whom she worked, though admittedly not Christian, were thrilled about her healing, while certain Christian friends and acquaintances seemed embarrassed and unbelieving when she explained the circumstances under which her dramatic recovery had been affected.

"Apparently some of my friends would be relieved to see me back on crutches," she said. "It's funny how unsettling a miracle can be."

As word of the prayer group spread, other interested church members found their way to it. In each meeting the Lord continued to meet people's needs and nearly everyone received the baptism in the Holy Spirit. However, in spite of regular announcements in church and a warm welcome for each new visitor, most of the congregation remained aloof. But whenever one or two would suddenly break and come, whether out of a real interest or simply a need, they inevitably found the power of God so captivating that they joined the group. For example, an eighty-four-year-old woman wrote the following observations to her minister son after attending several meetings:

"I can't begin to explain to you all that happens, but you can know when people drive twenty miles twice a week to attend a prayer meeting which begins at 8:00 p.m. and may last until nearly midnight, they have found something vital. Anyone who comes cannot help being deeply stirred, even as I have been, by the Divine love and power evident there."

Word of the Holy Spirit's outpouring quickly spread to other Disciple churches in Ontario, and at inter-church gatherings I would often be drawn aside by some layman who would express interest and appreciation for what was happening and share with me some experience of his own where God had moved miraculously in answer to prayer.

A quiet, grey-haired elder from another church stopped me at the coffee table after one such meeting to express his delight over Lilian's dramatic healing. Then he said, "Believing the way you do, I know you'll understand the story I'm about to tell you." He poured cream in his cup of coffee, then set the pitcher down on the table thoughtfully.

"My wife and I have always believed our Disciple churches are wrong to ignore the power of prayer. We *know* it works. When we were first married the doctor told us we could never have children. In fact, we went to several, and each one told us the same thing—that it was physically impossible. Well, we wanted children

129

desperately and were terribly disappointed. We went to our minister and asked him to pray with us that God would give us a child. He refused, saying we would just have to accept God's will and that if we wanted a child, to adopt one. Then he prayed God would give us strength to bear our disappointment.

"A few weeks later a healing evangelist came to our town, and we went to the services and asked for prayer. We knew the Bible said all things are possible with God, so we surrendered ourselves to God and told Him that if He blessed us with a child we would dedicate its life to Him. Ten months later our son was born. Next year he graduates from seminary and will be serving his own church."

I thanked the elder for sharing this remarkable testimony with me and drove home from the meeting that night reflecting sadly over the too-common story of unbelieving ministers.

Similar stories also came to light right in Hillcrest Church itself. One afternoon in my pastoral calling, I visited a woman whom I'd been told was very critical of our prayer meetings. I found I had been misinformed, for when I purposely steered the conversation around to the subject of prayer and told her a little of the group's activity, she smiled. "I can tell you a very personal story about God's healing in response to prayer."

Then she related how, over 20 years before, her first daughter had been born with a physical disability which made it impossible for her to digest food. The doctors could do nothing to correct the condition and after a lengthy hospital stay, sent the baby home with her mother. They warned that it would be only a matter of weeks until the baby died, and even if she were to live, she would be a complete invalid all her life. The little girl clung tenaciously to life, but after six months she weighed only eleven pounds and lay pinched and lifeless in her crib.

"I lived in constant dread," the mother recalled, "knowing that nothing could be done. Then one day while I was trying to feed my daughter, a neighbor lady came by. When she saw how the baby spit up every mouthful, tears came in her eyes. She said, 'We've got to do *something*—do you believe in prayer?' I said, 'I guess so.' 'I do too,' my neighbor replied, 'and so do the people in my little church. I'm going to ask our minister to call the congregation together Saturday night and we're going to spend the whole time praying that God will heal your baby.'

"Well, her church met for prayer on Saturday night like she said, and at midnight—when I gave my daughter her bottle—*for the first time in her life she drank three ounces of milk and kept it down!* From that time on she ate normally. After getting such a slow start, she didn't walk until she was two years old, but by the time she was six she was as bright and healthy as any other child in school. Today she's married and has children of her own."

"But didn't your own minister pray for the baby?" I asked. She shook her head.

"No, not for the baby. He came to see me twice after I brought my daughter home from the hospital, but he didn't pray for her, only for me—that I might have the courage to bear what God had placed upon me."

When ministers of the Gospel discourage their people from believing God's word and neither pray themselves nor urge their people to pray—*expecting God to act*—is it any wonder that miracles are still the exception rather than the rule in our churches?

Beautiful testimonies like these—coming to light after years of silence—only strengthened my determination that our prayer meetings in Hillcrest give the Holy Spirit every freedom and opportunity to manifest His miraculous power.

And we were amazed at the way the Holy Spirit exercised His sovereign control over the meetings. They were quiet and orderly, yet relaxed and informal, varying considerably in emphasis and content as the Spirit seemed to lead. We learned to look for and depend on that leading. At times the dominant note would be one of praise and adoration with much of the worship given over to hymn-singing and prayers of thanksgiving. Repeatedly we noticed that praying together "in the Spirit" —i.e., in tongues—lifted the worship to great heights. Along with praise there would often be interpretation of tongues and prophecy through which the Spirit comforted, instructed and strengthened the group.

Sometimes the presence of God in our midst was so overpowering we couldn't move. One night we sat unmoving in reverent silence for over an hour, literally in the grip of God's awesome presence. We seemed pressed to our chairs by some great Divine pressure. Later the word of prophecy came explaining we had been allowed to experience "the weight of His glory" that we might be continually reminded we were nothing and He was everything.

At other times the dominant note would be one of intercession. We frequently prayed for persons not present in the meeting. Someone would serve as proxy by sitting in a chair in the center of the room while others offered prayer. Time and time again we learned of health and strength returning to the one prayed for on the very evening prayer was offered. Once, as we interceded for a person with deep-seated psychological disturbances, we suddenly found ourselves speaking bold prayers of exorcism, commanding evil spirits to depart from the person in the name of Jesus Christ. The young man serving as proxy was startled by a vision which enabled him to see the demons leave. They appeared as figures with masked and tormented faces, casting furtive looks behind them as they scurried away. As the prayers ended he became aware of great peace surrounding the one for whom we had prayed. We later learned of striking improvement in the man's condition. I have no adequate explanation for that strange experience. The prayers of exorcism were unpremeditated and the startling vision unexpected. It was simply one more time when we served as instruments under the control of One who is sovereignly unpredictable.

As new members became receptive and asked, we would pray for their baptism in the Holy Spirit. Usually the first or second time such prayer was offered the one seeking would receive and speak in tongues. One girl, Margaret, seemed to be an exception. She had been coming for some weeks but seemed unable to respond to prayer. Then one night two new members appeared at the meeting, one of whom wanted prayer to receive the promised baptism. Several persons gathered around her chair while Margaret and the other visitor sat childlike on the floor at her feet. We began to pray, and in a sudden burst of glory, the Holy Spirit fell, not only on the woman for whom prayer was being offered, *but on Margaret and the other visitor as well.* They all began to speak in other tongues.

The Loving Presence of Christ was so real that had a hundred people come seeking Him that night, I felt every one of them would have received the baptism in the Holy Spirit. As the three began praising God in tongues, one man was given a vision of an angelic figure standing with hands outstretched in benediction over them. Another time he saw the same figure over a nineteen-year-old girl as she received the Holy Spirit.

Perhaps this is the place to stress that prior to this outpouring of the Holy Spirit none of us suspected God would manifest Himself in such supernatural ways. The people involved in the group were simply ordinary church people. They held jobs, kept house, reared children, fussed over car payments and dentists' bills and in no way considered themselves "other-worldly". Neither did they come to the prayer meetings "seeking visions". They came seeking God and to do battle with the forces of sin and sickness by exercising the power of Spirit-filled intercessory prayer.

Nevertheless, they began experiencing just what the prophet Joel prophesied and Peter repeated at the first

Pentecost: "I will pour out my Spirit upon all flesh, and your sons and daughters shall prophesy and your young men shall see visions and your old men shall dream dreams" (Acts 2:17).

One night we were seated in a circle praying quietly when one member glanced up and was nearly startled out of his wits to see the people fade from view and in their place appear a circle of bright blue shafts of flame. He later described the unusual experience in more earthy terms, comparing it to the circle of fire one sees coming from the burner of a kitchen gas stove. But we recalled that flames, or at least what appeared to be "tongues as of fire" were seen at the first Pentecost.

Some weeks later there was an incident so sacred it is difficult to record. We met as usual in the church parlor and had not been long in prayer until it was evident something very unusual was about to take place. God's Holy Presence was moving in our midst in a manner most tender and precious. Several young people were present, including Cindy, our 13-year-old daughter, who had received the Holy Spirit just the week before.

My wife, Alice, began a prayer of thanksgiving for the young people present and ended up praying an impassioned prayer for the saving of the youth of the world. The prayer seemed to voice the love and compassion of the Lord Himself. Then someone spoke in prophecy confirming that the Lord was manifesting Himself in our midst because of our faith and trust. We were told to fear no man but to keep looking to Jesus for the greater signs and wonders He was determined to perform. It wasn't so much the actual words of the prophecy which affected us as the overwhelming Love pervading the room.

Afterward a young woman, Irma Grace, shared with us what she had been privileged to see during those holy moments. During our prayers of praise, at the beginning of the meeting, the figure of Christ had appeared in the center of the group. Then, as Alice began her prayer for the youth of the world, Jesus had knelt beside her and wept as she prayed. He even reached out His hand and gently touched the knee of our daughter, Cindy, who was sitting next to her mother.

Half-frightened at what she was seeing, Irma Grace resolved she would not mention the vision, but at once Jesus walked over and stood in front of her in quiet rebuke. Instinctively she slipped from her chair and knelt at His feet in worship. Then He moved to the far side of the room and returned carrying what appeared to her to be a round straight rod some two feet in length. Standing in the center of the room He held the rod out horizontally before Him. All at once the rod started to unroll, and she became aware that He was holding a scroll. As the scroll unrolled, the prophecy began, and she knew it was the message contained on the scroll. As the prophecy ended the figure of Christ disappeared.

CHAPTER SEVENTEEN

Dreams and Visions

DURING THOSE DAYS I began to be greatly troubled over the possibility of opposition arising within the church. I was torn between the compulsion to encourage the prayer meetings in every way possible, while at the same time trying earnestly to maintain the proper pastoral relationship with the rest of the congregation, many of whom simply could not accept what was taking place. I kept remembering the attitude of the Board of Elders when I first shared my witness and felt at any moment the bubble might burst, leaving us up to our necks in controversy.

I doubted that such a powerful ministry could long be continued without Satan doing his best to throw a hitch in the whole proceedings. Spiritual revival seldom, if ever, comes without being followed by strong reaction and criticism. Attempting to minister to the whole church, I was caught on the horns of a real dilemma—how to promote spiritual revival and at the same time maintain congregational harmony. To this day I'm not convinced it can be done.

The devil has a sly way of hitting hardest where we're weakest. I hate being criticized. I would walk a mile out of my way to avoid even a small argument. Satan kept harassing me with fears of a church wrecked and divided by controversy, with the blame for the disaster, of course, resting squarely on my shoulders. It took a remarkable dream to convince me that my fears were not really justified and that, even if they were, God would be able to handle the situation. One night, following a trying and discouraging day, I tumbled into bed and some-time toward dawn had an unusual dream. Then I awoke with the power of the Holy Spirit surging through me like electricity. Immediately I secured paper and pencil and recorded the dream:

It is 5:00 a.m., June 1st, 1964. I have just awakened from a strange dream in which I found myself in the company of Spirit-filled friends aboard a ship. One woman, who resembled a member of my church, was wringing her hands in despair, claiming the ship would never make port because we were being cursed by evil powers. I urged her to share her fears with us, saying, "As you talk it will be like conversational prayer to God. You will be calling on the name of the Lord, and everyone calling on the name of the Lord will be saved."

"Our ship will pass through treacherous, storm-tossed waters, between dangerous cliffs and over perilous reefs," she said fearfully. "Even the winds and tides are evil! We will all perish!" And as she spoke it seemed we were experiencing the very perils she described. The ship beneath our feet was being driven and buffeted as she predicted. Then, with a grinding jolt we ran aground on some kind of bar or reef. I jumped into the ship's hold to wrestle with a mass of timbers, one of which had rammed into the cold, muddy bottom of the sea. It floated free as I tugged on it, and on the muddy end was a piece of paper which —a voice from somewhere told me—contained the conditions of the curse with which we were threatened.

This scene of the ship running aground and my wrestling with the timber in the hold repeated itself, again the scrap of paper appearing on the muddy end of the timber. Then I heard the woman speak again, "I don't care how bad it is; I want to know what is written on the paper."

I took the soggy scrap of paper in my hands. But as I held it the edges of the paper began to smoke and then burst into flames. I could not make out all it said, but saw it made vile and evil threats, promising heartache and tragedy for us and our families, even for our grandchildren. Somehow I knew the threat was aimed solely at those of us in the prayer group and I felt terribly afraid.

As I tried to read, one of the crew members standing

137

near us on the deck was suddenly transformed into a personification of Satan himself. Pointing his finger directly at me, he began quoting the curse recorded on the paper. His words struck me like an explosion, knocking me to the deck. Flat on my face, with fire and smoke and an evil stench billowing all around me, I felt powerless and helpless, drained of every ounce of strength.

But as I lay prostrate on the deck (I could actually feel the wooden deck floor against the palms of my hands and pressed against my cheek) I heard a calm, quiet voice of great authority and power speak. The voice spoke not only to me, but *through* me as well. *"Though a thousand fall at thy side and ten thousand by thy right hand, it shall not come nigh thee."* With sudden strength I pushed myself up from the deck and turned to face the devilish creature watching me. Smoke, sparks and a swirling evil aura surrounded him. I leaned forward as if into a strong wind and walked steadily toward him with my left hand extended as though pushing firmly against a wall. Then I heard myself saying with quiet authority, "I come against you in the name and power of the Lord Jesus Christ!" As I moved forward, the evil aura surrounding the figure began to diminish. All at once the smoke and sparks disappeared and the figure himself shrank into a small, elfin, rat-like creature, full of fear.

He tried to scurry into the ship's hold but I forbade him saying, "No, thou shalt not hide within the ship. Be thou removed and cast into the uttermost part of the sea." The pitiful little creature nodded his head and whined, "All right, all right," and rushing to the side of the ship, dived overboard. I turned to the others aboard and said, "See? He really had no more power than a water sprite."

With the creature gone, great quiet prevailed aboard the ship, and we found ourselves sailing in placid waters, heading into a peaceful harbor.

I am not a person normally given to vivid dreams, but the Holy Spirit used this one to bring me great comfort. From that time on, fear of opposition to the prayer meeting did not trouble me. Neither did such opposition ever arise.

We discovered in a rather remarkable way that the

power of the Holy Spirit can manifest itself even in small children. One prayer meeting night we had our five children with us, not so much by intent as by a shortage of babysitters. Cindy, the oldest, had become a member of the prayer group. Sharon and Glenn played quietly in an adjoining room, while the two little ones, Lisa and Laura, were in the church parlor with us. Lisa, our three-year-old, had awakened that morning with severe stomach cramps which would double her over with pain about every fifteen minutes. Remedies on hand proved ineffective, and we planned to have prayer for her healing.

We had hoped to wait until the meeting was well underway and our faith and expectancy built up, but when the cramps doubled Lisa over for the second time since our arrival, we decided to wait no longer. My wife held Lisa on her lap while several of the group gathered around for prayer and the laying on of hands. Baby Laura carefully surveyed the situation from the floor where she was playing and promptly set up a howl of objection to the special attention being given her older sister. To pacify her, one of the women in the group picked her up and sat down with her in a chair next to my wife.

Once more the unbelievable happened. As the prayer began, one of the girls sitting nearby was astonished to see the figure of Jesus appear behind the two chairs, standing with one hand resting lightly on the head of each of our children. As we began to pray specifically for Lisa's healing, He removed His hand from Laura's head and placed both hands on Lisa's head in prayerful benediction. Then He bent and kissed her on the cheek and was seen no more. Lisa immediately stopped her whimpering, laughed a delighted little laugh and squeezed a fuzzy toy she was holding. The cramps which had plagued her since early morning instantly disappeared, and as she slipped from her mother's lap her little face shone with a radiance not of this world. For weeks afterward she had an extra-special sweetness about her. At odd times during the day we would discover her singing hymns and carrying on conversations with Jesus. She was extra-affectionate and filled with more than an ordinary bright-eyed wonder at the world.

We left on our vacation the morning following her healing and drove to Texas to visit the children's grandparents. While in Wichita Falls, we were invited to an afternoon prayer meeting at the home of Mrs. C. H. Parker, a precious friend and leader of a women's prayer group which had prayed for our ministry through the years. It was a blazing hot afternoon in mid-August with the temperature well over 100 degrees when we drove across town to the Parker home. By the time we reached the house I had become so cross and irritable that Alice had difficulty in persuading me to go in for the meeting. Finally, I agreed—more to escape the heat than for any other reason—but I knew I was in no shape spiritually to minister or witness to that group. I confess this to make it plain that I take no credit for the miracle which followed.

Once inside the Parkers' lovely, air-conditioned home some of my composure returned. For no conscious reason—although obviously the Holy Spirit knew why—we had taken little Lisa with us to the meeting, leaving the other children with their grandparents. She sat quietly on my lap as the meeting progressed.

From the prayers and conversation it was apparent that a number of the women present were earnestly seeking the baptism in the Holy Spirit; therefore, I shared some of the happenings in our Toronto church, telling them how God had so richly blessed us by the Holy Spirit. When those seeking the baptism requested prayer, I left Lisa in my chair and stood behind the chair of the first candidate. As we began to pray, little Lisa suddenly hopped down, ran across the room and, reaching up, laid her little hands against the woman's cheek in a childlike benediction. Just how much her act contributed to the power in that prayer, I'm not sure, but all at once the heavens seemed to open. The Holy Spirit fell on *five* women who were seeking, almost simultaneously, and

140

they all began to speak in tongues. The descent of the Spirit was so sudden and overwhelming that I was momentarily stunned, then tears of joy started streaming down my cheeks as I lifted my voice in praise with the others. And there stood three-year-old Lisa, in the midst of all that praise and glory, smiling radiantly and very much at home.

One night in Toronto, when our prayer group was giving emphasis to prayer for healing, I was unexpectedly included. Every spring when the pollen count began to soar, like millions of others I contracted hay fever. Accepting it as my lot in life, I had accommodated myself to the discomfort and, between antihistamines, went sniffling and sneezing about my pastoral duties. That night, at the close of the meeting, one of the more observant members suddenly spoke up. "I think we should pray for the preacher's hay fever." Surprised and grateful, I took my place in a chair while prayer was offered. During the prayer I felt a kind of eerie, physical lightness, as if I suddenly weighed many pounds less. I thanked them, sneezed a couple of apologetic sneezes, and we all went home.

Two weeks later at the prayer meeting someone remembered and asked, "Preacher, how's the hay fever?"

"Hay fever?" I said, with a guilty start. Then, all at once I realized I didn't have any hay fever. I could not recall having had any hay fever since that night two weeks before when I had been prayed for. Ruefully, I admitted their prayers had been so efficacious that not only had my hay fever disappeared, but my awareness of it as well. The group chortled with laughter as I gave my red-faced testimony. I've had no trace of hay fever symptoms since.

At different times there were manifested in our meetings nearly all the nine gifts of the Spirit which Paul lists in First Corinthians 12. Then, too, there were the times when the Holy Spirit provided guidance in dramatic ways. One example of this started on a Saturday afternoon while I was mowing the parsonage lawn. It was a warm day and I welcomed the respite provided when our nine-year-old daughter, Sharon, brought me the evening paper. I sat down in the shade of the house and turned to the page listing the religious services. I had a long-standing hobby of looking for unusual sermon titles in the various church ads. However, what caught my eye this time was the announcement of a healing revival being conducted in a large evangelistic tabernacle at the west end of the city. I tried to continue my newspaper scanning, but my eye kept wandering back to that particular ad.

Suddenly, not quite knowing why, I said to Alice, "I'm going over to the Queensway Cathedral tonight— there's a healing revival on."

"How come?" she asked. "What about your rule not to go out on Saturday evenings?"

What Alice mentioned was quite true. We seldom accept invitations or make plans to go anywhere on Saturday nights. In our family there is just too much "getting-ready-for Sunday" to do.

I shrugged. "I just feel I ought to go, that's all."

An hour later I drove away from the house, almost angry with myself for giving in to a whim. "What's got into me?" I wondered as I picked my way through the Saturday traffic, heading in the general direction of the west end of Toronto. Then it occurred to me that I could help justify the trip by stopping at a hospital enroute, where one of our deacons lay recovering from surgery.

As I turned up the street to the hospital, I suddenly had the tingly awareness of the Holy Spirit's presence and all at once saw clearly what the whole business was about. I *knew* I was going to find the deacon in critical condition, and I *knew* the Lord wanted me to take his name to the healing service where special prayers could be offered for his recovery.

Entering the hospital, I quickly confirmed the accuracy of my guidance. The man had been transferred from the room where I had visited him two days before

142

and was in the intensive care ward under the constant supervision of doctors and nurses. A few hours before, acute complications had developed out of his surgery which now threatened his life. I was allowed to see him just briefly and explained that I was on the way to a service where special prayers would be offered for his recovery. He nodded gratefully and gasped, "I don't know anyone who needs prayer more than I do."

I arrived at the huge evangelistic temple to find the service already in progress. At the close of the sermon an altar call was extended for those desiring prayer. Dozens of people went forward to sit or kneel on the broad expanse of chancel steps. Picking my way to an un-crowded spot I sat down and prayed silently.

"Now, Lord, since all this is Your doing, I'm asking You to direct the healing evangelist to me." I felt a hand on my shoulder and opened my eyes. I gulped in aston-ishment as the evangelist sat down next to me and asked, "Brother, what is it you are seeking from the Lord to-night?" Quickly I acquainted him with the situation. At once he rose and called to the minister, asking him to secure the attention of the congregation. With me stand-ing in as proxy, the evangelist and minister laid hands on my head and, together with the entire congregation, offered prayer for my deacon's healing.

The special prayers that night stayed the hand of death, and then subsequent prayers of our own group carried him through two additional crises. He has since fully recovered and gratefully acknowledges that it was the power of God which saved his life.

Perhaps the most significant and inspiring thing of all about Hillcrest's experience of the Holy Spirit's power does not lie in the remarkable examples of the manifes-tations of supernatural gifts, but in the deep transforma-tion the Holy Spirit has wrought in the lives of those opening themselves to His power and presence. Those receiving the baptism in the Holy Spirit have found a strength and assurance in their faith which long years of conventional churchgoing simply never provided. They have found a reality in their personal Christian experience which transcends rational explanation, while furnishing them with testimony reminiscent of the New Testament itself.

One night at the prayer meeting we began by sharing what the Holy Spirit had been doing in each of our lives since we met last. As I listened to the quiet testimony of person after person and noted the deep love and affection which this unique fellowship had created, I thought, "Surely, this must be like the fellowship of the New Testament church, when the first Christians gathered in homes to worship God in the spirit and to share with one another the joy and wonder of the presence of the Living Christ in their lives."

One member began by telling how the Holy Spirit had led him to give his personal witness to a woman in the building where he worked, and how he ended up praying with her during the lunch hour they shared together.

A lovely young girl told of her attempts to help and understand a co-worker with whom she had severely quarreled in the past. She recounted how she had shared some of her recent prayer experiences with the girl and given her a small box of Bible promises as a token of her earnest desire to become friends. The girl received both the testimony and the gift with tears in her eyes and their strained relationship was well on the way to being healed.

A young man, planning a career in the ministry, told with joy of receiving an opportunity to preach an evening sermon in a small church in a nearby town and of bringing his first convert to Jesus Christ.

And so, around the circle it went, each person in turn confidently and joyfully sharing his own private miracle of the reality of the Living Christ within. Perhaps the greatest miracle of all was the fact that not one of those precious people would have been able, a year before, to make such a witness.

In the midst of those weeks of high spiritual excitement I received an inquiry asking if I would consider a call to a federated Baptist-Disciple church in Sharon, Pennsylvania. My first reaction was to ignore the letter, but common courtesy prompted me to reply. Considerable correspondence followed, which finally led to a visit to the church. We found the people sincere and cordial but saw little evidence of spiritual power.

During the drive back to Toronto, I remarked to Alice, "I really think I should write the chairman of the pulpit committee, telling him not to consider my name further. It's a nice church, but just not for us." Before I could write, however, a letter came stating that the congregation had voted to extend to us the call to become their pastor.

Many factors are involved when a minister considers a call to a new pastorate. Any sincere minister must try to evaluate his skills and talents in light of the particular needs and opportunities presented by the new church. Then, there is the practical side of things, such as salary, housing and schools for his children. Also there is the matter of timing. Is his contribution to the church he currently serves largely complete, or is he leaving unfinished work behind him? A minister is taught, both by training and experience, that these and numerous other considerations must be carefully weighed—weighing all these things carefully, we could see no earthly reason for changing churches.

However, we also knew that something more than earthly reasons must govern our decision. We needed clear guidance from God. So after the children were asleep that evening, my wife and I knelt in prayer and asked specifically that God's will be revealed to us. It was not long before the answer came, surprisingly and clearly. *We were to move.* No matter how indifferent we felt about the church in Sharon, and no matter how strongly we wished to remain at Hillcrest Church where the Holy Spirit was moving in such a powerful way, God let us know our work there was finished and that we were to accept the call.

Therefore, only about six months after the outpouring of the Holy Spirit began at Hillcrest, we bade the church goodbye. Word still reaches us that the Holy Spirit is continuing to move deeply and significantly in the lives of those whom the revival has touched. And ahead of us lay an even greater outpouring of the Holy Spirit upon the people we were being called to serve.

CHAPTER EIGHTEEN

God Did It Again

THE EAST SIDE CHURCH (Baptist-Disciples of Christ) in Sharon, Pennsylvania, is one of only a half-dozen federated congregations in the country where an American Baptist and a Disciples of Christ congregation have merged. But today the significant thing about East Side Church is not its unique combining of congregations but its demonstration of the faithfulness of God.

From our Toronto experience we had come to believe that God is always faithful to honor His Word. Therefore, if we were faithful to proclaim that Word in Sharon, and if the people in East Side Church were faithful to accept the Biblical message of Jesus' power to save, heal, provide and fill with the Holy Spirit, would not God confirm our trust and pour out His Spirit as He had done in Hillcrest Church? The answer is yes! In less than a year after leaving Toronto we were seeing a glorious repetition of charismatic revival in our new pastorate. God had done it again!

I want to describe the three steps in the pattern which developed—a pattern which I believe can operate successfully in almost any church. Here's the way it came about.

I. WE BEGIN TO BELIEVE GOD'S WORD.

The first step toward revival was the inauguration of a sustained program of Biblical preaching and teaching. Jesus once said, "Ye do err because ye know neither the Scriptures nor the power of God" (Matt. 22:29). His implication is clear. *To be ignorant of God's word is to be cut off from God's power.* In addition to Biblical sermons we began a Sunday evening Bible study, and it was through this study of God's word—particularly the New Testament—that our people began to realize how the will of God *for* us is inevitably linked with the Word of God *to* us. Our study of the New Testament quickly revealed three significant facts:

1. *Jesus ministered by the power of God.* He said, "The Son can do nothing of his own accord, but only what he sees the Father doing" (John 5:19), and "The words I say to you I do not speak on my own authority, but the Father who dwells in me does His works" (John 14:10).

2. *God the Holy Spirit empowered the lives of the New Testament Christians.* ". . . and they were all filled with the Holy Spirit and spoke the word of God with boldness . . . and with great power the apostles gave their testimony to the resurrection of our Lord Jesus, and great grace was upon them all" (Acts 4:31, 33).

3. *Jesus promised that His followers were to have the same power He had to do the same works He did.* "Truly, I say to you, he who believes in me will also do the works that I do; and greater works than these will he do" (John 14:12).

II. WE BEGAN TO PRAY FOR THE POWER OF GOD.

Out of this careful study of God's word there emerged a desire to test God's promises and prove they are still true today. So the second step toward revival was the birth of a weekly prayer meeting.

From sad experience I had learned the futility of trying to organize a prayer meeting as one might organize a committee. Instead, I waited patiently until a genuine hunger for the power of God expressed itself among the people.

It was many weeks after our Bible study had begun that one night, as Alice and I were praying at home, God revealed to us the time had arrived when His Holy Spirit would move with power among our people. "The plow-ing has been deep, the planting has been thorough, now the time for the harvest has come," were the words of the prophecy which came.

The following Sunday evening, several members approached me with jovial determination. "Why don't we begin a prayer meeting? Not just the ordinary kind we had years ago, but a really *vital* meeting where we seek the power of God for specific answers to our prayers."

"Through our Bible study we have diagnosed our spiritual sickness," one of our elders added, "now we think it's time to get on with the cure."

Of course, I was elated at this confirmation of the prophecy we had received only a few days before and at once proposed that we meet for the first time the following Tuesday. We did, and the prayer meeting began almost immediately to reap a harvest—but an *unexpected* one. In seeking Jesus' power, some members came to realize they had never really known Jesus Himself. Unaware that a vital, living relationship with Christ really existed, for years they had allowed knowledge about Jesus to substitute for communion with Him. Now they found Him to be a personal reality, and He became their Savior, Lord and Friend. As one amazed deacon commented, "I've been a member of this church for 27 years and no one ever told me such a wonderful relationship with my Lord was possible. Why haven't we heard of these things before?"

III. We began to experience the power of the Holy Spirit.

This combination of trust in God's word and earnest seeking of God's power through prayer resulted in the third step to revival—one which God Himself must take. His power began to produce the results the Scriptures promised. "You shall receive power when the Holy Spirit comes upon you . . ." Jesus said in Acts 1:8, ". . . these signs shall follow those who believe . . . In my name they will cast out demons, they will speak in

149

new tongues . . . they will lay hands on the sick and they will recover" (Mark 16:17). Just as in the days of the early church, and just as He had done in Toronto, God began to visit our people with repeated evidences of His miracle-working power.

"I simply didn't believe God would heal sickness today," exclaimed Mrs. Alice Silverthorn, professional musician and choir director of our church. "But I know better now, because it happened to *me!*"

Mrs. Silverthorn had been under a doctor's care for several weeks, suffering from a persistent throat infection which seemed to defy medication and which had forced her to give up plans to sing in our community-wide chorus' presentation of the Messiah at Christmas. During the Sunday morning church service on the day of the concert she poured out her despondency to God.

"Lord," she prayed silently, "if my earthly Father could, he would heal my throat. Why can't You heal it so I can sing again?" Suddenly, the thing she was sure could not happen, happened. As she testified later, "A strange, powerful vibration began in my throat and spread all through my body. When it ceased, my voice had returned and I was filled with a marvelous sense of well-being. I knew I had been healed."

That afternoon Alice gave a flawless performance of the Messiah, singing not only her own alto solo parts, but the soprano solos as well, after the soprano soloist failed to appear because of illness.

"I'll never doubt God's power to heal again," she says firmly today.

Another remarkable healing took place when Mrs. Pauline Davis—who had suffered from glaucoma for many years—received prayer with the laying on of hands. When Pauline returned to her doctor in a few days he examined her eyes carefully, shook his head and examined them again.

"I can't understand it, Pauline!" he exclaimed. "I don't know how or why, but your eyes are *fine*." Then he told her there was no need to continue the medication she had fully expected to use for the rest of her life.

Having had a measure of success with proxy prayer in our church in Toronto, we did not hesitate to use it in Sharon when the occasion made it necessary. Such was the case with Doris Lucas. Doris contracted a viral pneumonia against which all antibiotics proved useless. In a few days her condition became critical. She was admitted to the hospital, but grew steadily worse, and we knew that unless something happened she would lose her life.

On a Tuesday I visited her in the hospital, fighting back a sense of alarm over her wasted appearance. With more courage than I felt, I reminded her we would have special prayer for her at our prayer meeting that evening at the church. She nodded weakly and whispered, "I'll try to tune in."

That night one of our group sat in as proxy for Doris. Laying hands on her head we offered earnest prayer for healing. The sense of God's presence during our prayer was unmistakable. The next afternoon when I entered her hospital room Doris greeted me with a cheery hello. Her condition had improved remarkably.

"I'm glad to see you're better," I said.

"I certainly am," she smiled. Then she related how the evening before, while nearly unconscious and barely able to breathe, she suddenly sensed the presence of Christ in her room and seemed to hear His quiet voice say, "Stretch forth your hand." As she reached out her hand toward Him she found herself praying aloud, in unison with His voice, "Yea though I walk through the valley of the shadow of death, I will fear no evil, for Thou art with me . . ." and before the familiar psalm was finished she drifted off into a peaceful sleep. This experience took place a few minutes after 9:00 p.m. *at the precise time prayer had been offered for her at the church.* From that hour she began to mend.

A similar incident took place when another of our church members, Mrs. Walter Sheasley, who had been suffering unexplained dizzy spells and blackouts, became the subject for prayer. One night, as she sat in her living room watching television with her husband, we offered healing prayer for her at the church. Although she was unaware that we were praying, God reached across the intervening distance and touched her as we prayed. She sat straight up in her chair and turned to her husband. "Something wonderful just happened to me," she exclaimed. "I suddenly have the greatest sense of peace, and I feel sure I'm not going to have any more of those fainting spells."

Two weeks later Mrs. Sheasley was present with her husband at our prayer meeting to testify to her healing. In the months since she has had no recurrence of her illness. Shortly after her healing she and her husband were filled with the Holy Spirit.

These healing experiences have not made us any less appreciative of the marvelous work of doctors and surgeons, yet we often notice how the combination of medical treatment and prayer proves effective when medicine alone does not. Mrs. Eleanor Patterson, who was suffering severe pains from bursitis in her arm, sought prayer for healing in addition to the new medication given by her doctor. She was healed and returned to her doctor for examination. The doctor, who also suffered from the same condition, inquired how she felt.

"Just fine," Eleanor replied happily. "I'm completely well."

"You are?" came the startled reply. "That's funny. I'm using the same medication I gave you and it hasn't done a thing for me."

At times the spiritual climate in our prayer meetings has been such that people find healing without special prayer. One woman was instantly healed of a heart ailment during a prayer time when she joined in praying for someone else. Still another felt God's healing touch in the meeting one night, even though no one had prayed for her. Afterward she went home and removed a back brace she had worn for years. She's not worn it since.

When the Holy Spirit fell on the disciples at Pentecost, Peter said it was the fulfillment of the Old Testament prophecy that God would pour out His Spirit on all flesh and that "your young men shall see visions and your old men dream dreams." True to Biblical prophecy some of our people have experienced dreams and visions of an unusual nature. Angelic figures have been seen when various members were deep in prayer, both at the church and in people's homes. To Mrs. Olive Thompson, Jesus appeared in a dream and handed her a white gift, tied with gold ribbon. When she asked me what the vivid dream might signify, I explained that it is Jesus who gives the gift of the Holy Spirit. She requested special prayer with the result that Jesus graciously baptized her in the Holy Spirit.

On other occasions God has revealed ahead of time the identity of some His Spirit would bless. The night Mrs. Isobel Herster received the baptism in the Holy Spirit alone at home and began to praise God in a new language, a vision of an angelic figure appeared in her room. Superimposed on the figure she recognized the face of a certain young woman in our church. Within a few days this girl was also filled with the Holy Spirit.

One night while we were praying I was startled when there flashed in my mind a clear picture of one of our members. With the picture came an assurance that she would soon receive the baptism in the Holy Spirit. There had been no indication on her part of any interest in our prayer meeting, nor had anyone mentioned her name in prayer, so I was inclined to doubt what I had been shown. Yet within two weeks this woman experienced a remarkable healing and, along with her teenaged daughter, was filled with the Holy Spirit.

Our Tuesday night prayer meetings seem to provide the focal point for most of our spiritual power, but God often moves at other times and in other places. People have been healed, spiritually reborn, filled with the Holy Spirit and had prayers answered in our prayer meetings, in the regular Sunday services of the church and while praying alone at home.

Many can testify to being led in a remarkable way by the Holy Spirit. One of our deacons, Bob Miller—who was filled with the Holy Spirit years ago—is a member of the Gideons. At prayer meeting one night he reported how the Holy Spirit pressured him to drive several miles out of his way to stop at a new motel. When he walked in and introduced himself as a representative of the Gideons, the girl behind the desk gasped in surprise. She had just hung up the telephone after trying in vain to contact the Gideons. Bob's visit to the motel resulted in the immediate placement of 120 copies of the Bible. Since that experience Bob has been led by the Holy Spirit into a whole new ministry.

When I first came to Sharon, Bob was not a member of East Side Church. A quote from his own written testimony tells the circumstances which led to our meeting.

I had been active in church and Gideon work for years, but now this somehow seemed inadequate. It was not enough to do for my Lord who had done so much for me. In the summer of 1964 my telephone rang one Sunday morning. It was my married daughter, Gertrude. "Our car won't start," she said. "Will you come by and take us to church?"

"Be glad to," I replied. I had no Gideon assignment that morning, and I wanted to hear the new minister at my daughter's church.

The minister was Reverend Don Basham, and he had been preaching less than five minutes when I leaned over to my daughter and said, "This man has been filled with the Holy Spirit." The next day I went to the minister's study and showed him a copy of the Full Gospel Business Men's Voice Magazine and asked if he had ever seen one. He had. That was the beginning of a fellowship in the Lord which is still going on.

Bob invited me to attend the Full Gospel Business

Men's dinner meeting in Youngstown, Ohio, the following month. During the meeting I remarked, "Bob, won't it be wonderful when we have a group from the East Side Church who are open to the Holy Spirit and willing to share in a meeting like this?" Praise God! Less than a year later, twenty-five members of our church were present at this monthly Youngstown FGBMFI meeting, nearly all of them Spirit-filled.

Bob and his wife soon joined our church and took an active role in the ministry of prayer and witnessing. Bob works the afternoon shift in the big Westinghouse transformer plant in Sharon. One morning he came by my office to share a deep personal concern.

"I have a feeling that God wants to use me in a much greater way than He is now," he said, "and He knows I want to be used. Do you think there is any chance for a layman like me to become a minister?" Together we considered various possibilities, agreeing that with God all things are possible. Then we prayed for God to open new and wider doors of service for him.

A few Sundays later Bob had a Gideon assignment in a community church in New Lebanon, Pennsylvania, about 40 miles from Sharon. The following Tuesday night at prayer meeting he shared what happened.

"I gave my usual talk on the work of the Gideons and the people seemed receptive," he said. "But then, after church, a remarkable thing happened. Several people shook my hand and said, 'Will you come back and be our preacher?' I discovered the church had been without a minister for nearly a year. They had considered eight or nine men as candidates, but each had failed to get a majority vote. While gathering up my display Bibles I prayed silently, 'Lord, if this is an indication that You want to use me here, let the chairman of the pulpit committee say something to me.' Soon the church was empty except for one other man. He came over as I was packing my briefcase. 'I'm the chairman of the pulpit committee,' he said, 'and I was wondering if you would come back and preach for us again next Sunday, not as a Gideon but as a candidate to be our minister.' "

"I want your prayers tonight," Bob concluded. "I don't know if this is God's will for me, but if it is, I want to know. If it isn't and there is yet another door to open, I want this one slammed shut in my face."

We prayed and the Lord answered marvelously. Today, Bob has been pastor of the New Lebanon Community Church for over six months and the Holy Spirit has blessed his ministry with "signs following". People have been converted, healed and filled with the Holy Spirit—for revival has come to New Lebanon. Now, Spirit-filled members of that church are looking toward a nearby community as a possible mission field for establishing yet another non-denominational, Spirit-filled work.

CHAPTER NINETEEN

In Mysterious Ways, His Wonders to Perform

IN HIS EPHESIAN LETTER, Paul admonishes the people to "be filled with the Spirit, addressing one another in psalms, hymns and spiritual songs" (Eph. 5:18-19). We have found that the Holy Spirit often bestows talents and abilities where none existed before. For example, some of our Spirit-filled members have found themselves composing religious poetry and writing hymns of praise. One new poet keeps a notebook into which she copies each poem given her by the Holy Spirit, together with the date it was given. She has shared some of the poems at prayer meeting and their simplicity and spiritual beauty are inspiring. More recently some of the poems have been accepted for publication in religious magazines.

Mrs. Margaret Spinelli, to whom the Lord has been giving an abundance of both words and music, has purchased a small tape recorder into which she sings the hymns when they are given to her. Margaret has no professional musical training, so our choir director volunteered to help in the task of transcribing the music on paper. Increasingly, Margaret is finding opportunities to share her witness and unique musical gift with groups in other churches.

While the outpouring of the Holy Spirit at East Side Church has resulted in many demonstrations of God's supernatural power, there are also other less dramatic but equally significant evidences of His divine working.

157

Much to their delight, our people have found that the presence of the Holy Spirit enhances even the most ordinary tasks.

"I used to resent having to help with the preparation of dinners and refreshments at the church," one deaconess confided. "It all seemed so useless and insignificant. But now I find real joy in all my church tasks. And it's not that the jobs are so different. *I'm* different! The Holy Spirit has changed my way of looking at things. Now, even the ordinary things, I do *for Jesus.* And He makes all the difference in the world."

Another clear confirmation of the work of the Holy Spirit has been the quiet yet significant way attitudes have changed. People who never cared for one another have found genuine love and trust springing up between them. As one member confessed, "I used to keep a long mental list of the faults of other people in the church—all good reasons why I couldn't get along with them. But since receiving the Holy Spirit I find God simply gives me the ability to love people I couldn't love before."

The effect of the Holy Spirit's power among those who are receptive has been remarkable, yet for those who do not understand what is happening, it is still "church as usual". One of our deacons had a dream in which he saw Christ ministering to the sick and troubled in response to our prayers. But His ministry was veiled in a sort of mist and hidden from other church members who were standing nearby. They were completely unaware of what God was doing right next to them.

In spite of this, however, we have noticed a marked deepening of spiritual content and meaning in the overall program of our church, even among those not consciously a part of the spiritual awakening. As one teacher in our church school was heard to say, "I don't know why, but everything about our class seems to be going better this year. The children not only seem to be learning more, but they are more reverent as well."

One of the more remarkable aspects of this gracious outpouring of God's Spirit upon our church has been that the impact of it, though profound, remains quiet. This in itself is something of a miracle, since many times revival or spiritual renewal is accompanied by much strain and tension and no little pain. I believe our good fortune in being able—thus far—to avoid such disharmony is the result of careful obedience to the leading of the Holy Spirit. God seems constantly to remind us that witnessing to His power must be done in a gentle and loving manner. Repeatedly, persons have been checked by the Holy Spirit and kept from the hasty or ill-timed word. As a result we have seen the lives of dozens of people touched by God, yet with little criticism or complaint from the unaffected members.

We are quick to admit that our study of the Scriptures and practice of prayer have not provided us with all the answers. Neither is the baptism in the Holy Spirit an automatic solution to all spiritual ills. At times our prayers seem to avail nothing, with the conditions and people we pray for remaining unchanged. And in a few cases we have been disappointed to find a person who has been greatly blessed by the love and power of God retreating back into old habits and customs. We are also learning that simply because God moves graciously in answer to prayer on one occasion, this does not guarantee that subsequent problems and illnesses may not arise. It is apparent that He wants us to remain *constantly dependent upon Him,* and that He intends our trusting His Word and living in His presence to be a daily discipline.

Meanwhile the list of blessings bestowed upon our people by God's miracle-working power continues to grow. We have developed a real sense of expectancy as we wait to see what the power of God will do next. As one radiant woman remarked after church recently, "I don't know whether that inspiring service marks the end of one glorious week or the beginning of another." A companion said, "I sometimes wonder what we talked about and what we did with ourselves before we were filled with the Holy Spirit. The love and power of Christi seem to fill my whole life now, and I find myself wanting to share Him with anyone who will listen."

The Holy Spirit's ministry in East Side Church has, on occasion, reached out to bless those of other churches, enabling us to develop strong ties of love and prayer with them. The following story is illustrative of this.

We have a young woman, Arlene, in our church who as a child was disabled by a crippling disease. Since she had no family to look after her, the welfare board placed her in the home of one of our elderly widows. Recently, however, this woman became ill herself and could no longer care for Arlene. When the new home where Arlene was placed proved unsatisfactory, it appeared the welfare board would be forced to return her to the state hospital. Arlene asked me for both help and prayer in finding a place where she could live and be happy.

"I'll be praying for myself, too," she said earnestly. "I don't want to go back to that old hospital!" At prayer meeting we lifted her need before the Lord.

Upon inquiry I found the names and addresses of two local families who seemed to be possibilities. I knew neither family and neither home answered when I telephoned. However, the next afternoon during my pastoral calling I found myself on the street near one of the addresses. Stopping in front of the house, I knocked on the door. No answer. I knocked again. Still no answer. Five more times I knocked and waited. Finally the door opened. Behind the screen door the interior of the house was dim and I could barely make out the form of a woman standing there.

"Yes, what is it?"

"Are you Mrs. Ruth Wortman?" She nodded and I introduced myself, explaining the purpose of my call. It was awkward talking through the screen door, but she made no move to invite me inside. Finishing my explanation I waited for her reply. Long moments passed and she said nothing. Finally, I blurted out, "You are the Mrs. Ruth Wortman who is interested in caring for someone in her home, aren't you?"

At that, she started, visibly. "Oh, my goodness! I don't know what came over me!" Then she swung the screen door wide. "Please, Reverend Basham, come in! How stupid to keep you standing outside."

Going inside, I at once found Mrs. Wortman to be a charming, motherly woman in her middle years, her gentle face graced with the clear, wide eyes of a child. A few minutes of conversation also convinced me that she was a woman of lovely Christian character.

"I hope she is able to take Arlene," I thought.

As we spoke further I casually mentioned how, at our prayer meeting, we had been praying about Arlene's situation. Ruth's face lit up radiantly. "Oh, do you believe in prayer?"

"Indeed I do," I responded. "And so do many in our church. At our prayer meetings we've experienced some remarkable answers to prayer."

The woman literally clapped her hands in delight. "*Wonderful!* Now I can tell you so much I was afraid to say before." She then revealed that she had been praying specifically for God to send her a disabled young woman to look after and love.

"I have no children of my own, but I have lots of love to give, and I feel the Lord has given me a ministry of caring for needy people. From what you tell me of Arlene, I believe she's exactly the person I've been praying for!"

Then she smiled. "Now that I know you better, I want to tell you that I don't normally keep people standing outside my door like that. It was just that your coming gave me such a start! You see, I've been working nights at a rest home, so I sleep during the day. I went to sleep this noon praying that God would send me someone to look after. I was asleep when you knocked, and when I finally opened the door and you told me why you were here, I thought I was dreaming. When I realized I was awake, I was so speechless over having the answer to my prayer come knocking at my door, I just stood and stared. Please forgive me!"

161

I laughed. "Well, I don't normally knock seven times at a door, either. But the Lord just kept me pounding away until you heard me." I reminded her of the story in Acts 12 where the disciples were praying for Peter's release from prison. When an angel freed him and he came knocking at their door, they thought he was a ghost at first and wouldn't let him in. We had a good laugh together over the similitude between the two incidents.

As Ruth told me about her ministry of caring for people, I learned that as a practical nurse she had demonstrated a unique gift in caring for her patients; a gift recognized by a number of local physicians. On several occasions, seemingly hopeless cases brought to her by the doctors had been nursed back to health.

"It's the prayer more than anything else," she assured me, "I *know* God heals through prayer." I then asked her how this ministry of praying for people began, and she responded with a remarkable story.

"Years ago, when I was a girl of eighteen, my oldest sister, Goldie, lay in the hospital dying of cancer. The night before she died I was sleeping in a chair beside her bed when she woke me up. 'Ruth,' she said, 'the Lord Jesus just came and stood by my bed and told me that if you'd lay your hands on me and pray, I would get well.' "

Ruth paused and shook her head sadly at the memory. "But I didn't have the courage to pray for her healing. I began to cry and I said, 'Oh, Goldie, I can't do that! I'm not good enough to pray like that. I'm afraid!' My sister said, 'All right, Ruth. If you don't think you can, then I guess you can't. I know I'll die if you don't, but I don't mind. I've seen Jesus and I'm ready.'

"Well, I didn't pray and the next day Goldie died. But I never forgot what she said. Of course, some claimed that she was out of her head and imagining things. But I knew she spoke the truth. I just didn't have enough faith to trust God.

"Years later my husband also lay in the hospital dying, only in his case it was pneumonia. When the doctor said he had only a few minutes left to live, I sent for my brother-in-law. 'Pete,' I said, 'do you remember how —before Goldie died—Jesus told us if we prayed she would be healed? Well, we failed Goldie, but I don't intend to fail my husband. You stand at the foot of his bed. I'm going to lay hands on him and we're going to pray for God to heal him.'

"By this time," Ruth continued, "my husband's breathing had almost stopped. A horrible grey pallor had spread over his face and arms. In fact, the doctor was out in the hall filling out his death certificate. But as I laid my hands on his chest and prayed, something seemed to strike his body and it almost jerked off the bed. He had been in a coma for hours, but his eyes snapped open and for a moment he looked right at me. Then he closed his eyes, that awful pallor began to disappear, and his breathing became normal. When the doctor came in a minute later, he swore. 'My God! What's happened to this man? A minute ago he was dying and now he's sleeping normally!'

"In a few days we took Ralph home from the hospital and to this day the doctors can't explain what happened to him."

After sharing with me several other dramatic instances where God had brought health and healing to her and others for whom she'd prayed, Ruth changed the subject and asked me about our prayer meeting. "Do your people believe in the baptism in the Holy Spirit and speaking in tongues?"

"We certainly do," I replied.

Ruth nodded her head emphatically. "I thought so! I believe in it too, but the folks in the little church where I go . . . they believe in prayer, well enough, but they don't hold with speaking in tongues. But I know the Bible teaches that it is one of the gifts of the Holy Spirit—just like healing. I've never spoken in tongues, but I know it's real."

Now I saw that God had more than the one purpose in bringing us together. Inwardly praising Him, I said, "Sister Ruth, I believe the only reason you haven't re-

163

ceived this blessing is because no one has come along to explain it to you and pray with you. Would you like to receive the baptism in the Holy Spirit right now?"

Ruth nodded and listened intently as I explained how we receive the Holy Spirit within simply by offering a prayer of invitation and how we manifest His presence by praising Him in the language He provides. Then we began to pray.

With beautifully simple faith, Ruth prayed the prayer of invitation, opened her mouth and began worshipping God in other tongues.

"See how simple it is?" I exclaimed. Her eyes wet with tears, Ruth smiled. "I know now I could have had this a long time ago if I had known how to respond to the Spirit's prompting. He's been wanting me to praise Him in tongues for a long time and I haven't known how to yield to Him."

At the close of a glorious two hours, I left Ruth's home rejoicing in the Spirit and praising God. Today, Arlene is happily settled in the Wortman home where she is loved and cared for as if she were their own daughter. When I shared Ruth's testimony with the members of our prayer group, it blessed and thrilled them as it had me. And I share it here in the confidence that it will continue to bless all who read it, confirming once more that Jesus Christ still lives, still heals and still baptizes in the Holy Spirit today.

CHAPTER TWENTY

Your Personal Experience

THE WITNESS OF THIS BOOK has been that the miraculous power of God is as truly available to us today as it was in the Apostolic age. The Book of Acts in our New Testament reports not so much the "Acts of the Apostles" as the acts of God *through* the Apostles. The early Church came "face up with a miracle", not just once but repeatedly, and the demonstration of God's supernatural power was not so much the exception as the expected thing.

Those of us involved in the present world-wide recovery of the miraculous in the Church are convinced that the particular miracle which begins God's supernatural power and blessing pouring into our lives is the baptism in the Holy Spirit.

Toward the end of his account of our Lord's life, the Apostle John said, "Now Jesus did many other signs in the presence of the disciples, which are not written in this book; but these are written that you may believe that Jesus is the Christ, the Son of God, *and that believing* you may have life in His name" (John 20:30,31). In something of the same manner, the testimony of these pages has been shared "that you may believe that the risen, glorified Jesus is still baptizing in the Holy Spirit and that *receiving*, you may have supernatural power in His name."

We believe that no Christian's spiritual progress can be complete without this enpowering. Therefore, no book dealing with the power of God can be complete without endeavoring to help the seeking Christian personally to experience the fullness of the Holy Spirit in his life. This chapter is written for this purpose. If you would like to receive this blessed promise of our Heavenly Father, may we suggest that you first read the entire chapter, then at your own appointed time, in the privacy of your prayer corner, re-read the chapter, carefully following each outlined step until the promised baptism in the Holy Spirit and the miracle of praising God in a new language becomes your own joyous possession. Praise God! He is *faithful* and will not let your desire go unfulfilled.

A minister driving through busy city traffic was silently thanking God for His help in a pastoral call just completed, when suddenly he found himself praising God in a strange new language.

The religious editor of a newspaper sought the gift of the Holy Spirit for years without success until, in the privacy of her own bedroom, she followed the advice given by a Spirit-filled friend earlier in the day and opened her mouth to praise the Lord with "sounds". As soon as she uttered the first syllable in faith, the Holy Spirit poured a whole new fluent language of praise into her mouth.

A college professor was contemplating his need for more of Christ's power as he stood in the kitchen of his home opening a can of soup. Opening his heart to the Holy Spirit, right then and there he began to praise God in an unknown tongue.

A woman in Baltimore, Maryland, accepted the invitation of a pentecostal acquaintance to attend a revival service. Suffering from poor health, she went to the meeting to seek prayer for healing. During the lengthy service, however, her attention wandered until her friend nudged her and whispered that the evangelist was calling forward those who desired prayer. Expecting prayer for healing she moved to the appointed seat. The congregation began to pray, and after a few moments she began to feel strange and "tingly" all over. As she described it, "Suddenly my tongue began to thrash aroun

166

in my mouth and I began to weep as a great flood of compassion welled up within me. All at once I found myself speaking aloud words and syllables I could not understand. I felt gloriously alive with power and knew something wonderful had happened to me." She had been completely unaware that the invitation had been for those desiring to receive the baptism in the Holy Spirit and did not understand until later what had happened to her.

Examples of this type could be listed almost indefinitely, but these are sufficient to illustrate how the Holy Spirit is freely given to those who are open to receive Him. These incidents also make it clear that there is no single technique or method of preparation essential for receiving the baptism in the Holy Spirit. Let me hasten to say, however, that there is one *prerequisite* which *is* absolutely essential. *If you have not already done so, you must accept the Lord Jesus Christ as your personal Savior.* By no means should anyone who is not a believing Christian pray for baptism in the Holy Spirit! But if you are a believer, then you can and should enter this deeper dimension of spiritual living.

There are two basic ingredients: the readiness of our Lord Jesus to baptize the believer in the Holy Spirit and the desire and readiness of the Christian to receive baptism in the Holy Spirit. The Bible teaches that this experience is given freely by grace—to help us move ahead into the highlands of Christian victory and warfare—and is not an attainment or reward based on some supposed degree of holiness. However, if you need guidance in your seeking and asking, or if you have been seeking and not yet received, the following steps will make it easier for you to cooperate with the Lord. I am firmly convinced that any earnest Christian, by following these steps as outlined, will receive the Holy Spirit in a matter of minutes. Are you ready?

I. *Find a time and place for quiet prayer and meditation.*

While it helps to be in the presence of a group of Spirit-filled Christians who can instruct, encourage and pray with you, such a fellowship is not essential. In fact, many earnest, seeking Christians who felt self-conscious in the presence of such a group have received the baptism in the Holy Spirit in the privacy of their own homes, just as you may.

So find a place where you can be quiet and undisturbed for a period of prayer and waiting upon the Lord. The physical surroundings are not important—just so long as you can be quiet and comfortable. You may sit, kneel, or take whatever position that will encourage your sense of reverence and spiritual expectancy.

II. *Re-read the Scriptures where the Holy Spirit is promised.*

And it shall come to pass afterward. that I will pour out my Spirit on all flesh; your sons and daughters shall prophesy, your old men shall dream dreams and your young men shall see visions. Even upon the menservants and maidservants in those days. I will pour out my Spirit (Joel 2:28-29).

I (John) baptize you with water for repentance, but he who is coming after me mightier than I, whose sandals I am not worthy to carry; he will baptize you with the Holy Spirit and fire (Matt. 3:11; also Luke 3:16 and Mark 1:8).

And these signs will accompany those who believe: in my name they will cast out demons; they will speak in new tongues (Mark 16:17).

And I tell you, ask, and it will be given you; seek, and you will find; knock, and it will be opened to you. For every one who asked receives and he who seeks finds, and to him who knocks it will be opened. What father among you, if his son asks for a fish, will instead of a fish, give him a serpent; or if he asks for an egg, will give him a scorpion? If you then, who are evil, know how to give good gifts to your children, how much more will the heavenly Father give the Holy Spirit to those who ask Him? (Luke 11:9-13).

And behold, I send the promise of my Father upon you; but stay in the city until you are clothed with power from on high (Luke 24:49).

He who believes in me, as the scripture has said, "Out of his heart shall flow rivers of living water." Now this he (Jesus) said about the Holy Spirit, which those who believed in him were to receive (John 7:38-39).

And I will pray the Father, and he will give you another Counselor, to be with you forever, even the Spirit of truth, whom the world cannot receive, because it neither sees him nor knows him; you know him, for he dwells with you and will be in you (John 14:16-17).

These things I have spoken to you while I am still with you. But the Counselor, the Holy Spirit, whom the Father will send in my name, he will teach you all things, and bring to your remembrance all that I have said to you (John 14:25-26).

But when the Counselor comes, whom I shall send to you from the Father, even the Spirit of truth, who proceeds from the Father, he will bear witness to me (John 15:16).

Nevertheless, I tell you the truth: it is to your advantage that I go away, for if I do not go away, the Counselor will not come to you; but if I go, I will send him to you (John 16:7).

I (Jesus) have yet many things to say to you, but you cannot bear them now. When the Spirit of truth comes, he will guide you into all the truth; for he will not speak on his own authority, but whatever he hears he will speak, and he will declare to you the things that are to come. He will glorify me for he will take what is mine and declare it to you (John 16:12-14).

And while staying with them he (Jesus) charged them not to depart from Jerusalem, but to wait for the promise of the Father, which, he said, "you heard from me, for John baptized with water, but before many days you shall be baptized with the Holy Spirit" (Acts 1:4-5).

But you shall receive power when the Holy Spirit has come upon you, and you shall be my witnesses (Acts 1:8).

And Peter said to them, "Repent, and be baptized every one of you in the name of Jesus Christ for the forgiveness of your sins; and you shall receive the gift of the Holy Spirit. For the promise is to you and to your children,

169

and to all that are far off, every one whom the Lord our God calls to him" (Acts 2:38-39).

Now that you have read and accepted the above passages which clearly reveal that the baptism or gift of the Holy Spirit is meant for all, I want to point you to a seemingly unrelated, but highly important and helpful passage of Scripture, Matthew 14:22-31:

> Then (Jesus) made the disciples get into the boat and go before him to the other side, while he dismissed the crowds. And after he had dismissed the crowds, he went up into the hills by himself to pray. When evening came, he was there alone, but the boat by this time was many furlongs distant from the land, beaten by the waves; for the wind was against them.
> And in the fourth watch of the night he came to them, walking on the sea. But when the disciples saw him walking on the sea, they were terrified, saying, "It is a ghost!" And they cried out for fear. But immediately he spoke to them saying, "Take heart, it is I; have no fear."
> And Peter answered him, "Lord, if it is you, bid me come to you on the water." He said, "Come." So Peter got out of the boat and walked on the water and came to Jesus; but when he saw the wind, he was afraid, and beginning to sink he cried out, "Lord, save me." Jesus immediately reached out his hand and caught him, saying to him, "O man of little faith, why did you doubt?"

This Scripture contains the story of how Peter sought and experienced a miracle. It is significant for you, because to receive the baptism in the Holy Spirit is to experience a miracle. By examining this story and identifying yourself with Peter and his actions you can be greatly helped to receive.

When Peter saw Jesus approaching on the water he said, "*Lord if it is you,* bid me come . . . " Peter wanted assurance that the miracle he sought was in accordance with the will of God for his life. Many people today ask, "How do I know it's God's will that I receive the baptism in the Holy Spirit? The Scriptures listed previously should make it abundantly clear that the Lord *does* desire to bestow this gift on everyone. So accept His will for you in this matter with joy and anticipation, knowing that His invitation to receive applies to "*you* and your children, and to *all* that are far off."

Now, let us also note that Peter said, "Lord, if it is you, *bid me come to you on the water*." Peter *knew* he was asking the Lord for a miracle; asking Him for what no man on earth could grant. Only God could provide, by His supernatural power, the means for Peter to walk on water. By the same token, the baptism in the Holy Spirit and speaking in tongues is a miracle which no man on earth can grant. Only God, by His supernatural power, can fill you with His Holy Spirit and enable you to speak in tongues.

But Jesus told Peter to "Come", because He knew God's power would sustain Peter on top of the water. Jesus tells you to "Receive", because He knows God's supernatural power will fill you and enable you to speak in tongues.

By his willingness to come in response to Jesus' invitation, Peter, in effect, was saying, "Lord, if you say I can do it—if you say I can walk on the water—I trust you to make it possible." So also, you who are seeking the baptism in the Holy Spirit must say, "Lord, if you say I can receive—if you say I will speak in tongues—I trust you to make it possible."

III. *Pray the prayer of invitation.*

In a simple, fervent prayer, ask Jesus to fill you with the Holy Spirit. You may use a prayer like the following:

> Lord Jesus Christ, I believe with all my heart that the baptism in the Holy Spirit is meant for me. Just as I trust you for my eternal salvation, so now do I trust you to give me your Holy Spirit with the evidence of speaking in tongues. I now open my life to receive the fullness of your Holy Spirit within. Thank you, Lord Jesus, Amen!

IV. *Receive the Holy Spirit within.*

Having prayed your prayer, *believe* and *act* on it. Know that at this very moment the Holy Spirit is moving into your life in a new and powerful way in answer to your prayer. Claim your answer! In a conscious act of surrender, let Him have full control of your body, mind and spirit. Be confidently aware of His presence within.

At this point you may actually *feel* the presence of the Holy Spirit, physically. His presence may come as a warmth enveloping you, or as a silent powerful Presence enfolding you. You may experience a tingling sensation or a gentle vibration as if touched by an electric current. But even if you feel nothing, rest quietly in the confidence that the Holy Spirit is *now* coming upon you in power and is about to furnish you with a new language of prayer and praise to God.

V. *Receive and speak the language the Holy Spirit gives.*

This is the point where your faith and trust must resolve themselves into action. In the Biblical story of Peter's miracle, it is at this point that Peter acted boldly and in faith, even as you must. The Scripture simply states, "So Peter *got out of the boat and walked . . .*" These few words hold the key! They reveal how the miracle took place, and when you understand them, they also hold the key to your speaking in tongues.

Before the miracle of God could take place, Peter had to do his part. Jesus did not lift Peter over the side of the boat, Peter stepped out of the boat and began to walk. It was an act of faith and courage, but it was a purely human act! The miracle of God's power was not made manifest until *after* Peter got out of the boat. The miracle was not that Peter walked, but that God held the water firm under his feet! Read the story carefully. The Lord did not carry Peter. Peter, on his own, stepped over the side of the boat and began to walk. It was Peter walking, not God carrying him. If Peter had waited for the power of God to lift him out of the boat and float him across the waves to Jesus, he would still be in the boat today!

So it is with the miracle of speaking in tongues. The miracle is not that you speak; you do your own speaking just like Peter did his own walking. You are to speak out with your own lips and voice, just as Peter stepped out of the boat with his own legs and feet. The miracle comes when, as you open your mouth to speak, you trust God to furnish you with a new language of praise—words and syllables in a new and unknown tongue. Peter walked, and in doing so, trusted God to hold the water firm under his feet. You are to speak, trusting God to give you a new language with which to praise Him. Lift up your voice in faith, trusting that *as you begin to speak,* it will be in a new and beautiful language you have never heard before.

Do not hesitate. Do not be afraid to open your mouth and speak. Refusing to speak out in faith leaves you like Peter sitting in the boat. As long as he sat there and did nothing, there was no miracle. As long as you keep silent, there will be no miracle of speaking in tongues.

When the Holy Spirit fell at Pentecost (Acts 2:4) ". . . they were all filled with the Holy Spirit and began to speak in tongues as the Spirit gave them utterance." Note carefully what happened on that occasion. *They* were filled and began to speak; the Holy Spirit didn't speak, the Apostles spoke. The Holy Spirit "gave them utterance", or provided the words. The 120 themselves, with their own lips and tongues, did the speaking. The miracle was the Holy Spirit's furnishing them with languages they had never learned.

As you allow the Holy Spirit to furnish you with this new language of praise, remember, you will not understand the language—it will be an "unknown tongue" to you. But do not let this stop you from speaking . . . your responsibility is not to understand but to speak out in faith.

The Holy Spirit may prompt you to speak in any one of several different ways. If you have been praising God in English, you may find your speech becoming difficult, your voice stammering. Yield to this stammering and the new language will form itself easily. Or you may

173

experience the beginning of this "unknown tongue" by having the Holy Spirit insert strange-sounding syllables and words in your mind. Do not dismiss this as mere imagination; you are under the control of the Holy Spirit and the words are from Him; Speak them out in faith. Speak out boldly, even though you may feel foolish doing so. Peter must have felt foolish walking on water, too.

VI. *Keep on speaking in faith.*

Once you have begun to manifest the presence of the Holy Spirit within by praising God with the new language He has given you, it is important for you to continue to speak until you become completely familiar and comfortable with your new spiritual ability. It may be at this point that your greatest doubts will come. Satan will use your conscious mind, the old "mind of the flesh" to tempt you to reject the whole experience.

Here is the time to profit by Peter's mistake. We have seen how Peter's bold act of faith in stepping over the side of the boat initiated God's miracle. But then we read how Peter took his eyes off Jesus and stared at the wind-swept water. ". . . but when he *saw the wind*, he was afraid, and beginning to sink he cried out . . ." (vs. 30). In other words, when Peter let go of his faith and began an intellectual analysis of the impossibility of what he was doing, he began to sink! Obviously, his fear and doubt came from Satan, not from God; for when Jesus reached out and caught him, He chided Peter for his fear. "O man of little faith, why did you doubt?" (vs. 31).

So it is with your speaking in tongues. You may be so very self-conscious when you first begin to speak in tongues, and it may be so different from what you anticipated that you will wonder if it is all real. *It happens this way with so many people that we can almost reduce it to a law!* You will feel strange and you will have doubts. After all, you're travelling unknown territory. Nothing in your past experience can match it. You're like a babe

174

toddling in a new land. You may even stutter and stammer like a baby, at first.

Beginning tongues often sound very much like baby talk. But this results merely from a natural hesitancy born out of a new and altogether strange experience. So you stammer, so what? "With stammering lips and another tongue will He speak to His people" (Isaiah 28:11, 12). Paul quotes from this passage in Isaiah while teaching on tongues (I Cor. 14:21). You are in good company!

Don't make the mistake Peter made! The miracle of your speaking in tongues *is* from God, and the doubts which may rise to plague you are from Satan. Remember Paul's statement, "For if I pray in tongues my spirit prays *but my mind is unfruitful*" (1 Cor. 14:14). In other words, you are not supposed to understand with your intellect what your spirit is praying in tongues. Satan, however, will use the "unfruitfulness" of your intellect— the fact that you can't "make any sense" out of the tongues—in an attempt to discredit the miracle which is taking place, just like he used Peter's rationalization about the impossibility of walking on water to cause Peter's faith to falter.

Therefore, disregard your doubts; disregard feeling strange; keep your eyes fixed on Jesus as you worship—and praise Him. The more you continue to praise Him in tongues, the firmer you will become established in this new spiritual dimension, and the more fluent will be your praise.

We have noted with delight the rich variety of beautiful and worshipful languages in which Spirit-filled friends offer praise to God. But while some people, from the moment of their receiving, demonstrate great fluency in tongues, others seem to speak only a few words or syllables. We've found, however, that a bold faith, coupled with a sense of abandon, or willingness to be humbled for Christ's sake, quickly establishes a greater fluency in tongues. Often the seeming inability to pray freely in tongues is simply a lack of trustful boldness.

Years ago, a group of us prayed—seemingly without success—for a young wife to receive the baptism in the Holy Spirit. The following night she returned, at which time she found glorious liberty in praising God in tongues. Then she shared with us how, as we had prayed with her the previous evening, her mind had been filled with words and phrases she did not understand. But she was too shy to speak them aloud. All the next day, as she busied herself with her housework, the Holy Spirit continued to pour such an abundance of unknown words through her thoughts she could think of nothing else. When we prayed with her the second time, the torrent broke loose, much to her great joy. Many a person seems at first to share a like reluctance to speak, but the Holy Spirit continues to move in a loving and gracious manner until enough confidence comes to trust Him and to speak out.

The blessed experience of the baptism in the Holy Spirit and speaking in tongues ushers you through a spiritual doorway into all manner of spiritual blessings. Remember, this is not an end, it is a *beginning*. A whole new supernatural world of spiritual experience lies ahead. Potentially, you have become a powerful and effective witness for Jesus Christ, so don't let Satan rob you of God's best. Keep your eyes on Jesus, hold fast to the Word of God, and soon you will be firmly grounded in your new life in the Spirit.

"Thanks be to God for His inexpressible gift!"

CHAPTER TWENTY-ONE

And Still the Spirit Moves

ONE NIGHT, FIFTEEN YEARS AGO, a group of us sat around the fireplace in the large manor house at Koinonia Foundation, sharing testimonies and praying about the future. One of God's joyous saints, Rufus Moseley, was in the group. Half serious and half in jest I said, "Brother Rufus, prophesy for us. What do you see ahead for us and our country?"

Rufus was silent for a little while, staring thoughtfully into the fire. I felt certain he was praying. When he finally spoke it was with simplicity but great earnestness. "Whenever I pray about the future," he said, "the same answer always comes, and it is this: *Everything and everyone inside the Spirit of Jesus will become better and better, while everything and everyone outside will become worse and worse.*"

The truth of Rufus Moseley's prophecy becomes more evident year by year. Where—outside the Spirit of Jesus—is there reason for optimism today? Outside His Spirit there seems little in store except confusion, waste, indulgence, immorality, bitterness, lawlessness, hatred, violence, war, terror and mounting despair. All the brilliance of our technological achievements, all our increasing prosperity and material abundance we find to be sullied and tarnished, betrayed by the corresponding lack of personal integrity, self-discipline and loving concern for others. In the words of Emerson, "*Things* are in the saddle, and ride mankind." Our land of plenty writhes in the throes of spiritual and moral bankruptcy, and all the while overhead—like the sword of Damocles —hangs the threat of atomic annihilation.

Caught in her own struggles against impotence, agnosticism and worldliness, even the church seems powerless to help. As doubt and skepticism increase within her walls, we see an almost wholesale abandonment of the basic tenets of the Christian faith. Brilliant theologians and ministers argue persuasively that either "God is dead", or that "we can get along very well without Him". Outside the Spirit of Jesus, we do indeed stand on the brink of chaos.

But thanks be to God, the first half of Rufus Moseley's prophecy is equally true! Everything and everyone within the Spirit of Jesus *is* destined to become better and better. And to the task of lending evidence in support of this glorious truth, this book has gratefully addressed itself.

Alongside the rise of rebellion and lawlessness in the world (which Scripture itself clearly foretells), [1] alongside the great "falling away" from revealed Christian truth, we find God moving swiftly and dramatically to restore to the Church all the supernatural gifts and powers promised in the New Testament. We are witnessing an outpouring of the Holy Spirit "upon all flesh". There *is* hope! There *is* a way out! For out of the moral and spiritual wreckage of our day, *God is moving to claim a people for Himself.* And even the briefest glimpse of this great move of the Holy Spirit quickens and gladdens the heart.

Some great ministries have caught the nation's attention and imagination, such as those of Billy Graham and Oral Roberts. The work of these servants of God is familiar to every home in America. The literary success of the best-seller, *The Cross and the Switchblade,* has shown a startled and grateful public the miracle-packed "Teen Challenge" ministry of David Wilkerson among the young drug addicts of New York City's lower east

1. See Matthew 24:1-14

side. With a sustained and daring faith in the power of the Holy Spirit to set the addict free, this ministry has multiplied many times over in the past few years, and today Teen Challenge Centers exist in many of America's major cities.

Another well-publicized move of the Holy Spirit is the growing ministry of the Full Gospel Business Men's Fellowship International. To describe its growth is to describe a miracle.[2] The miracle began with the grandparents of California dairyman Demos Shakarian, founder of the FGBMFI, and dates back to events in Armenia, Old Russia, where in 1855 a Spirit-filled prophet of God foretold the coming destruction of the Armenian community and warned the families to move out of the country. By 1900, in obedience to the vision, all the Christian families had left Armenia. Many, like the Shakarians, immigrated to California. In 1914, at the beginning of World War I, the Turks invaded Armenia bringing with them the terrible slaughter which more than fulfilled the prophecy given sixty years before.

The FGBMFI was born in 1953 following a vision given Demos Shakarian in which God showed him how the Holy Spirit was to be poured out on the business men of America. From the establishment of a single chapter in Los Angeles, this fellowship has grown in just fourteen years until today there are over 400 chapters, meeting in all major cities and nearly every state in the United States, plus a growing number of chapters in cities abroad.

The primary means of promoting the aims of the FGBMFI is their monthly magazine, *The Full Gospel's Business Men's Voice*. Beginning in 1953 as a 12-page pamphlet, the magazine has grown with the organization and today each 32-page issue has a printing of nearly 300,000 copies, not counting those published and printed in foreign countries. The magazine contains moving

2. The details of this amazing story are recounted in the booklet, *The Shakarian Story*, by Thomas R. Nickel, published by the FGBMFI.

testimonies of people whose lives have been dramatically changed by the power of the Holy Spirit.

Another remarkable ministry which has sprung up only recently is that of Inter-Church Renewal: This organization seeks to open a door of utterance for many newly Spirit-filled ministers of all denominations across the land. Their spiritual seminars for ministers are becoming an outstanding contribution to spiritual renewal.

The printed page always plays an important role in any widespread revival, and certainly that is true today. A growing number of outstanding books are exercising wide influence, some even pushing their way into the "best-seller" bracket. *They Speak with Other Tongues* by John Sherrill, *I Believe in Miracles* by Kathryn Kuhlman, *Aglow with the Spirit* by Robert Frost, *Come Away My Beloved* by Frances J. Roberts and *The Release of the Spirit* by Watchman Nee are but a few examples.

Also several fast-growing independent periodicals are available, such as *Testimony* magazine, *Recovery* magazine and *Acts* Magazine.

The new *Acts* magazine is unique in that it is primarily a news magazine, with over fifty contributing editors, endeavoring to graphically portray what God is doing worldwide. A beautiful fifty-two page magazine, *Acts* will undoubtedly have a tremendous impact.

Yet another outstanding phase of testimony is the ever-growing ministry of tape. *The Inspirational Tape Library* in Phoenix, Arizona, under the direction of Dr. Gordon Beckstead, is the prime example of this important contribution. Thousands of tapes are available on a low-cost rental plan or are for sale through the Library's *Tape-of-the-Month* Club.[3]

3. Information on the ministries referred to in this chapter can be had by writing Voice Publications, Box 672, Northridge, California 91324.

But significant as these ministries are, a greater miracle—unnoticed by the public and carefully ignored or disparaged by most church denominations and their leaders—is to be found in the birth of literally thousands of prayer groups in homes and churches all across the nation. Into these tiny havens of spiritual power an increasing number of spiritually hungry church members are finding their way. There they encounter the Living Jesus as Saviour, Healer and Baptizer. There they experience the same transforming power of God which characterized the early church.

A classic example of such a charismatic church fellowship is the one which a number of our own church members attend. It meets every Saturday night from 8:30 p.m. until midnight at the Neshannock Presbyterian Church in nearby New Wilmington, Pennsylvania. Dr. Victor Dawe, Neshannock's Spirit-filled pastor, began the meeting three years ago as a small prayer group for his own people. Today, however, each meeting draws from thirty to sixty people from ten or twelve congregations representing at least a half dozen denominations. Sharing in the ministry of this remarkable group, we have witnessed conversions, healings, deliverance from demonic powers, personality transformations and manifestations of tongues, prophecies and other spiritual gifts as the Living Jesus reveals His power and presence to those seeking Him.

A typical meeting begins with a tape recording of a message by some recognized spiritual leader. Then follows a time of sharing and testimony, often interspersed with prayer. Midway in the meeting there will be an enthusiastic song service led by the Spirit-filled sexton of the church, whose formal education ended with the third grade. The singing is accompanied on the piano by a woman who holds a Ph.D. degree in music and serves on the faculty of nearby Westminster College.

Later comes a time of deep and concentrated prayer

in the Holy Spirit. It is from this time of praise, petition and intercession that miracles often emerge. Only God knows the full extent of the influence of this one charismatic group on the lives of the Christians who come from as far as fifty miles away to share in its vital ministry.

Other smaller, but equally powerful groups meet in private homes, like the Friday night meeting in the home of Miss Flo Dodge, in Pittsburgh's North Hills. Here too, the charismatic pattern repeats itself, with the Holy Spirit blessing the participants through deep and prayerful study of the Word of God, through prophecy, tongues and interpretation, or perhaps a word of wisdom or knowledge, as well as through healing and the baptism in the Holy Spirit.

The spiritual potential of such house prayer meetings is immense. Thoreau once wrote of a small New England village which consisted of only a few homes and a handful of people. "Nevertheless," he added, "it is a village where a great man may be born any day." The same is true of these house prayer meetings. Though small, great new moves of the Holy Spirit may come to birth within their walls.

Take, for example, the time we met at Flo Dodge's home in early February of this year. Two young Roman Catholic men visited the meeting that night. Both were instructors in theology at Duquesne, the large Roman Catholic University in Pittsburgh. They had heard of the new "charismatic" dimension of prayer and came to the meeting in Flo's home to see for themselves what took place. Before the meeting ended both asked for and received prayer for baptism in the Holy Spirit.

Alice and I returned home to Sharon that night pleased to have a part in praying for our new Roman Catholic friends but without the slightest awareness of what the Holy Spirit had begun in that time of prayer. The first word of results came three weeks later via a letter from a Spirit-filled commercial artist friend, Jim Prophater, who with his wife Katherine, had also been present at the meeting.

Dear Don,

Greetings in the precious name of Jesus! We have so much to share with you that I can't begin to put it all into a letter. I hope we will be able to see you personally before too long.

There has been such a tremendous move of the Holy Spirit here in Pittsburgh that it is making our heads swim —because we are right in the middle of it. Remember the two young instructors of theology from Duquesne who received the Holy Spirit at Flo's when you were here last? Well, Ralph Keifer, the tallest of the two, went home that night so full of the Spirit that he was bursting. He told his wife about it—I guess until the wee hours of the morning —prayed for her and she received. Since then they brought one of the priests at Duquesne. He was open and since has also received the baptism. Then they took thirty Duquesne students on a week-end retreat, for the purpose of studying the first four chapters of Acts. They had an upper room experience and *twenty or more received the Holy Spirit!* Back on campus they have been praying fellow classmates through to receive. The instructors have prayed other teachers through to salvation. They even called Bishop Wright, informed him of what is happening and—praise the Lord!—he too is open.

They recognize the need for instruction, and we have been helping them. Friday night we went to hear testimonies of some of the students. We took our pastor (Assembly of God). They have invited him to come to Duquesne to instruct the new Spirit-filled Christians. Can you believe that? Nothing is impossible with God! But He sure shakes us up sometimes when He moves so quickly and in such power.

There are many souls crying out for spiritual fellowship and ministry in prayer in the South Hills area now. They have come to us from several different sources. So it looks as though the Lord is leading us to open our home again for prayer as we did before. We are just waiting on Him.

We all here send our love to all in your precious family. The way things are moving these days it may not be long until we are together with Jesus in the air. Hallelujah!

Yours with love in Him,
Jim

Soon the Duquesne prayer meetings were reaching fifty or sixty students and several faculty members as well. But the move of the Holy Spirit did not stop with Duquesne. Ralph Keifer, on a visit to the Notre Dame campus at South Bend, Indiana, gave his testimony to friends there. A few days later another Duquesne professor who had received the Holy Spirit through Ralph's ministry, also visited Notre Dame and not only gave his testimony but prayed for nine of his friends to receive the Holy Spirit. Although this man had not—up until that time—spoken in tongues, nevertheless within a week six of the nine friends he prayed for found themselves praying in unknown tongues in their private devotions.

Through the testimony and prayers of the nine, the outpouring of the Holy Spirit spread, and in the weeks that followed dozens of students, both from Notre Dame and adjoining St. Mary's College, received the baptism in the Holy Spirit. A number of theology professors and priests also received and joined ranks with the students in the burgeoning charismatic meetings where over a hundred Spirit-filled persons now gather for prayer and praise. Visiting Catholic students from Michigan State University joined the meetings, received the baptism and returned to their own campus to establish a strong charismatic group. Also a group from Notre Dame traveled to Iowa State University, and there, too, the Spirit moved among the Catholic students.

In the past several weeks the "pentecostal" Catholic students and their meetings have been widely reported in the national press. Reading an article in a copy of the Youngstown, Ohio *Vindicator*, which described the charismatic meetings at Notre Dame, St. Mary's, Michigan State and Iowa Universities, I found myself praising God Who had taken what began as a simple prayer of faith over two sincere young men who were seeking more of Him, and seemed to be turning it into a spiritual renaissance of major proportions among the future leaders of the Roman Catholic Church.

Once aware of this twentieth-century "return to the charismata", wherever one looks the power of the Holy Spirit is in evidence. From the Atlantic to the Pacific, from Canada to Mexico and beyond, the Holy Spirit continues to move.

In New York you can visit the charismatic nerve center located in Rev. Harald Bredesen's First Reformed Church in Mt. Vernon, where seeking Christians from all over the country and from all walks and professions have found spiritual reality. Opera singers, composers, journalists, priests, psychiatrists and ministers have received the baptism in the Holy Spirit there. Harald, whose ministry has been featured in national magazines and national radio and TV programs, has traveled the world over as charismatic emissary to churches, colleges, seminaries and mission stations.

In Florida you can witness the powerful ministry of a group like the "Committee of Forty" (the actual number greatly exceeds that!) in Ft. Lauderdale. Headed up by a gentle, Spirit-filled Episcopalian stockbroker named Eldon Purvis, this loose-knit fellowship numbers among its leaders professional men from nearly every field. Men like attorneys John Stanford, Boyd Anderson, Paul Manning and Jack Musselman; men like veterinarian Nelson Makinson, insurance executive Jay Cheshire, tax assessor Bruce Hill and airline pilot Carell (Buddy) Cobb. Men whose greatest joy in life is to bring persons to a saving knowledge of Jesus Christ and into the fullness of the baptism in the Holy Spirit. These are men who consider their major vocation to be witnesses to Jesus Christ, and their professions but a means to provide them with the financial resources to further their service for the Lord.

The wives in the group have organized a daily "chain telephone ministry" involving thirty Spirit-filled women. Within minutes after the first word of any serious need, every member of this band of feminine prayer warriors has been informed and is offering earnest and believing prayer in regard to it. Out of this one ministry alone

185

there have come miracles of healing which amaze local physicians.

The Committee of Forty has been responsible for numerous prayer and Bible study groups scattered throughout the Miami-Ft. Lauderdale area. Also, a major contribution to the deepening spiritual life of their community has been a series of three-day retreats called "Holy Spirit Teaching Missions", held every four months over the past two years. In these retreats Spirit-filled leaders from near and far are invited to witness and teach men and women from a wide divergence of church backgrounds concerning the current work of the Holy Spirit.

Recent word from Ft. Lauderdale reveals how this vital group is now moving in faith toward a vast expansion in its ministry. Following a highly successful experimental TV program on the charismatic movement, the Committee of Forty is now waiting expectantly for final approval of their license application for a new Christian television station.

Then, across the country in Seattle, Washington, you can visit St. Luke's Episcopal Church, a prime example of what can happen when the power of the Holy Spirit revives a dying church. In 1961 St. Luke's was a struggling mission church consisting of a handful of discouraged parishioners who were ready to close the church doors for good. Then Father Dennis Bennett came, bringing the fire of the Holy Spirit with him. Today St. Luke's is the strongest church in the diocese, a burgeoning congregation of over seven hundred members, one-third of whom have received the baptism in the Holy Spirit. Thousands of people from all over the nation have visited St. Luke's Friday night "information meetings" to gain first-hand experience in the charismatic dimension of Christianity. For the express purpose of helping people receive the baptism in the Holy Spirit, St. Luke's has a trained group of about seventy-five counselors who are experienced in witnessing, answering questions and praying for those seeking a deeper walk with God.

Such ministries are but a few of the larger, more spectacular outworkings of this revival here in the United States; but for each of these mentioned there are hundreds more scattered across the nation, and in scores of foreign countries, quietly lighting fires of spiritual renewal and preparing the people of God for the end-time ministry which nearly every sensitive spiritual leader in this country testifies is nearly upon us.

Billy Graham declared recently that he is convinced we are on the verge of a sweeping revivial and that this age will end, as it began, with signs, wonders and miracles, to the glory of God. In fact, it is being prophesied daily that as the climax of this age approaches there is to be a revival of gifts and powers of the Holy Spirit which will far exceed that which the church experienced in the days of her beginning. We are crossing the threshold into a day wherein we shall see the words of Jesus literally fulfilled: *"Truly, truly I say to you, he who believes in me will also do the works that I do, and greater works than these shall he do . . ."*

Epilogue

How does a story like this one end? It doesn't. The narrative may stop, but the work of the Holy Spirit continues. In reviewing what I have written, I am startled to find that almost half the incidents related here had not even taken place when I began writing nearly four years ago. And for every incident included in these pages, others have been omitted. Left over are whole completed chapters, plus rough material more than enough to fill another book. The Holy Spirit is moving so rapidly these days that written testimony cannot keep up with His miraculous acts. Yet we desperately need more books of testimony, more contemporary books of "Acts," so that the world may come to know what God is doing. And they are on the way. Even now others are putting pen to paper, or sitting before typewriters, pounding out their own stories of the power of God at work in their lives.

In these pages I have shared the story of our own search for spiritual reality and the results of that search up to now. Much of that story centers around the baptism in the Holy Spirit, an experience which millions of Christians have discovered opens the way to "unsearchable riches" that are in our Lord Jesus Christ. I make no claim to understanding fully all that is implied in this experience. However, one does not have to understand fully to receive. We walk by *faith*, not by sight nor understanding. I have not written as a theologian, nor have I based my testimony on a carefully developed body of Christian doctrine. I have written merely as an amazed and grateful witness.

I read my New Testament and thank God for what happened in the lives of believers back then. Then I look around me at the changed lives, listen to the vibrant testimonies of reborn, Spirit-filled Christians and my heart sings out, "Thank God, it happens *now!*" I am surrounded by living chapters in God's continuing Book of Acts!

But certainly this is not all God has in store. May God forgive us if we stop with the baptism in the Holy Spirit or any other "experience". There is no end to your spiritual quest and mine. Ahead lie more precious realms. Ahead lie spiritual adventures far grander than any we've encountered, adventures which will call for a deeper death of the old man we once were, in exchange for greater triumphs of the new life in the Spirit of Jesus Christ. And everywhere the world over, people are waiting to receive the good news of what we find.

The path may be straight and narrow, but it is also glorious and ascending. The only life worth living is the life that leads to the summit. *We are meant to climb —not coast!* Like Paul, we are to "Press on toward the goal for the prize of *the upward call of God in Christ Jesus.*"[1]

Why camp in the foothills when the summit still beckons? Let us get on with the climb. We stand to gain everything worth having and to lose nothing worth keeping. How can we fear, knowing *He* is with us? How do you know high mountain shale is slippery until you've started at least one avalanche of your own? Only the man who has made the climb has the right to say, "It's a long way to fall."

There is more than one kind of height, more than one kind of space. Exploring the outer reaches of God's physical universe is no more important than exploring the inner reaches of God's spiritual universe. One must be matched by the other.

One day soon a man launched from the earth by rockets will reach the moon. But that achievement won't

1. Philippians 3:14

really solve anything. *For our ultimate destiny does not lie with the man we put on the moon, but with that Man we put on the Cross.* It is *He* who will yet have the final word.

So let us begin! If crucifixion comes, let it come, as it did once before—on a hill. On ground higher than where we began.

"You shall receive power when the Holy Spirit has come upon you, and you will be my witnesses . . ." [2]

Acknowledgments

PERHAPS SOME BOOKS are written for which the author may take sole credit, but this is not one of them. I have had the help and encouragement of many people. Among them are Dr. Robert Walker, editor of *Christian Life* magazine, Dr. Victor Dawe, pastor of the Neshannock Presbyterian Church in New Wilmington, Pennsylvania, and my journalist brother, Col. Hal Basham, professor of Air Science at Ohio State University, each of whom read the manuscript and made many helpful suggestions.

I must also acknowledge my great debt to the late Dr. G. Edwin Osborn of Phillips University whose gentle spirit and wise counsel meant so much to me. He was the first to insist this testimony be made public.

I also wish to thank the various members of the Hillcrest Christian Church in Toronto, Canada, and the East Side Church (Baptist-Disciples of Christ) in Sharon, Pennsylvania, plus a whole host of other individuals who have been willing to have me share in print how God's love and power has blessed their lives.

I am indebted in a special way to Spirit-filled

2. Acts 1:8

friends like Irma Grace and Gunther Sawitzki, Robert W. Miller, Cosmo de Bartolo and Alfred White.

Last of all, my heartfelt gratitude goes to my wife Alice, and our five children—Cindy, Sharon, Glenn, Lisa and Laura—for their patient and willing sacrifice of hundreds of hours of companionship with a husband and father who seemed interminably hunched behind a clacking typewriter and piles of manuscript paper.

To all these, and most of all to our Lord Jesus Christ whose miracle of grace in my life compels this witness, I owe an everlasting debt.

Don W. Basham